This book is dedicated to Thomas Douglas Pickford

Front cover: Macclesfield Parish Church

By the same author:

Myths and Legends of East Cheshire and The Moorlands	£5.95
Magic, Myth and Memories, in and around The Peak District	£7.95
Staffordshire: its Magic and Mystery	£7.95
A Portrait of Macclesfield	£6.95
Macclesfield, So Well Remembered	£7.95
Macclesfield, Those Were The Days	£7.95

Also of interest:

Dark Tales of Old Cheshire (Angela Conway)	£6.95
Strange South Yorkshire (David Clarke)	£6.95
Myths and Legends of Cornwall (Craig Weatherhill & Paul Devereux)	£6.95
Ghosts, Traditions and Legends of Lancashire (Ken Howarth)	£7.95
Mysteries of the Mersey Valley (Peter Hough and Jenny Randles)	£7.95
Shadows: a northern investigation of the unknown (Steve Cliffe)	£7.95
Supernatural Stockport (Martin Mills)	£5.95

All of the above and many more Sigma Leisure books on regional heritage, local history, country walking and cycling are available from your local bookshop or direct from the publishers: If ordering by post, please add £2 p&p for a single book (two or more books are post free). Our address is:

Sigma Leisure, 1 South Oak Lane, Wilmslow, Cheshire SK9 6AR

A free catalogue listing over 100 of our publications is available. Please write to the above address or phone us on 01625 - 531035.

CHESHIRE:
its magic & mystery

Doug Pickford

SIGMA
Leisure

Copyright © D. Pickford, 1994

All Rights Reserved. No part of this publication may be reproduced, stored in a retrieval system, or transmitted in any form or by any means - electronic, mechanical, photocopying, recording, or otherwise - without prior written permission from the publisher.

Published by Sigma Leisure - an imprint of
Sigma Press, 1 South Oak Lane, Wilmslow, Cheshire SK9 6AR, England.

British Library Cataloguing in Publication Data
A CIP record for this book is available from the British Library.

ISBN: 1-85058-422-2

Typesetting and Design by: Sigma Press, Wilmslow, Cheshire.

Cover design : The Agency, Wilmslow

Printed by: Manchester Free Press

Dedication and Acknowledgments: There are many who have assisted me in the production of this book in countless ways. Thanks and gratitude go to my wife, Hilary, a psychic medium who has seen what has not been certain and who has helped, encouraged and advised and who has been my companion on adventures throughout the highways, byways, fields, moors, peaks and plains of Cheshire. Considerable assistance has been given by Derek Hulland, the Cheshire historian and one of the finest characters in the Palatine, and by Mr and Mrs John Ennion of Bunbury Moss who welcomed us as strangers and from whom we departed as friends. There are many others to whom thanks are gratefully given, including Maurice Winnell.

Contents

1. Introduction — 1
   Beelzebub and The Antrobus Soul Gang — 4
   Mystical Story-teller — 6
   Celtic Egg Myth — 12

2. Worshipping the trees — 16
   Bawming the Thorn — 18
   Healing Oak — 23
   Wild Floralia — 26

3. A-Maying in The Land of The Green Man — 32
   The Goodly Fires — 38
   Where's Jack? — 43
   Cheshire's Green Knight — 47
   The Green Head — 49

4. Dance of the Witches — 57
   The Edge of Darkness — 59

Reflections of Images	63
A Pinch of Salt	68
The Curse of Death	74

5. Be weer of The Buggins — 80

A Hunting We Will Go	83
A Prestbury Tale	86
The Haunted Town	91
More Ghosts than Grains of Salt	98
Bottling or Laying a Ghost	102

6. Dragons and the sleepers underfoot — 105

Following the Dragon Paths	119
The Gallant Venables and St Michael	129
Meeting a Sheila-na-gig	132
Dragons of stone and wood	134

7. Realm of the fairy folk — 139

Carrying the Stones	145

8. Grinning cats, black dogs and panthers — 152

From cats to dogs	155

9. Magic water, mysterious stones	**161**
The Cult of Water	162
Healing waters	170
Power of the White Water	173
Rivers of Life and Death	176
Magic of the Stones	179
Index	**185**

Cheshire: its magic and mystery

Cheshire as it was, before local government reorganisation

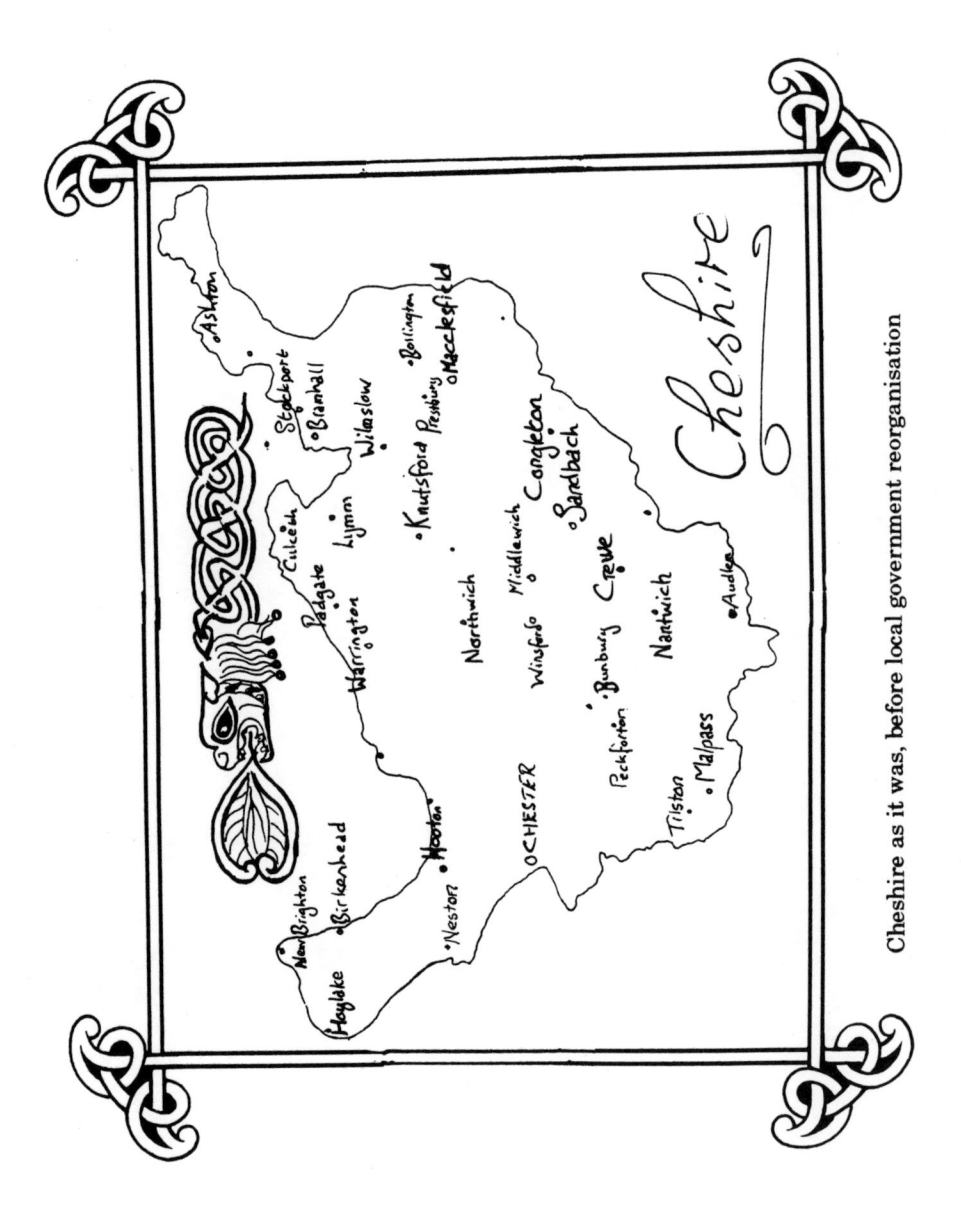

1

Introduction

The October mist blanketed the high hedgerows as Hilary and I drove along the Holmes Chapel to Knutsford road on our way to see the Antrobus Soul Gang perform their age-old ritual. But we were late and we knew they as soon as they met up at the Antrobus Arms they would set off for hostelries near and far. Only after meeting together would they decide where they were to visit on that night. If we did not get there in time then there was no way of knowing where they were or where they were going and we would have the devil of a job tracking them down. We would have to wait another year before seeing such characters as The Black Prince and the Letter In, along with Beelzebub and the 'Oss.

So what was to be done? If we travelled our usual route then time would run out ... so we had to put our faith in Cheshire.

We decided that we should be guided to Antrobus. I turned the car at the next side road, went left, right, straight over the crossroads, right, left and then ... we were in Antrobus. Our journey along the dark and misty lanes had taken a little over ten minutes and the way by the main road would have taken well over twice as long. I had not known where we were driving through because sign posts were at a minimum but certainly knew *why* we were going the way that we were and knew where we were heading to. What had been our guide? Faith? Luck? Co-incidence? Perhaps all three but most certainly faith, because we knew that Cheshire would not let us down. As we travelled on automatic pilot along those lanes it was never a question of were we going in the right direction because it always felt that we were on the right track and it was never a question of would we get there at the right time, because we knew.

And that sums up Cheshire. It feels right.

It has always felt right. The Palatine of Cheshire is a land where the Spirit of the Place is very much alive and it is a land where magic can still work and where the mysterious still occurs.

Lewis Caroll, the mystic, wrote of *Alice's Adventures in Wonderland* and he most certainly knew of Cheshire's wonders when he penned this masterpiece; many of them are contained within his works if you look carefully. Yes, there is the Cheshire Cat but there is much more. The Soul Gangs of All Hallows Eve are within those pages if you seek them and the White Rabbit and the Queen of Hearts are characters from the salty soil of Cheshire. He was a man of Cheshire and he knew much more about what makes the place tick than he said in his works. Cheshire is a land where the fairy folk still linger and where the witches still dance; it is a land where the ghosts still haunt and the Green Man still resides.

So why should this be? Why is this marvellous, magical, mystical Palatine so different from other places?

The answer surely lies very much within the people of this County themselves for it is they who have kept alive so much that has been lost in other parts of England and Wales; it is they who have retained their love of the place and it is they who have retained the Old Knowledge.

There are two Cheshires – the one we see upon its surface and the one that lies underneath it. Much of the County has been forced to change because of industrialisation, commercialisation and urbanisation and because of what is, laughingly, termed progress. There are huge new highways that do not now follow the old tracks and there are towns that have been spawned from nothing – towns without a heart beating within. There are artificial boundaries that have not always been there and there are mammoth mines that have eaten into the earth as we have gone in search of salt, coal and minerals. But Cheshire, despite all this, is one of the most beautiful Counties within this land and, even more importantly, it still retains its magic and wonder and, just like a beautiful woman, it retains its mystery.

There are still places that can be visited where the Earth Spirit dwells and there are still magical places that can be viewed where the past is still alive.

What, you may be asking, is this "Earth Spirit" I'm pontificating about? And, while we're at it, what's so "magical" about the place and what' so "mysterious"?

I would blame you but little for asking these questions and perhaps I should try to throw more light onto the darkness:

Where else, for instance, would it come as no surprise that a hare guides your way to a fairy ring?

Where else would trees still be worshipped and used to heal?

Where else would the legends of dragons still live on?

Where else would the memories of the Celtic Holy Men be retained?

Where else would there be one of the most powerful natural energy points of the entire world?

And where else was created by a giant?

Where else but Cheshire?

This is the land where myths and legends are made and where there are few secrets for those who ask the right questions. Cheshire is a Wonderland in its own right and is a place where much exploration can take place. There are still adventures to be had just as Sir Gawain found when he hunted across the Wirral for the Green Knight and Venables the Dragon Slayer discovered at Moston when he met the beast with six claws. This is a land of mermaids, monsters, buggins, boggarts, wizards and witches, dragons and werewolfs and some of them are still alive.

Come with me within the pages of this book, if you will, and let us look at some of the more unusual aspects of this mysterious County. This is not a history book and it is not a geography book; it is a book of exploration for those with an inquiring mind.

Hopefully, some of you will be familiar with previous works of mine when I have explored East Cheshire and the Moorlands, the Peak District and Staffordshire in the same manner. Those who have read those books will know that I make a point of not accepting everything that is said and done. Just because a legend has been around for a good few hundred years does not, in my mind, mean it is correct. I enlist the aid of divining rods to show where the earth's energy lines are. I am also greatly and considerably aided by my wife, Hilary, who is a talented Medium. And, just as in all my previous works, I have had the joy of meeting some wonderful people who have also assisted me in the exploration of this county and who have become firm friends during this time. If, along the way, some discoveries have been made, then so much the better.

Exploring Cheshire – a county I thought I knew before I set out on this quest but was soon to realise I most certainly did not – has been a delight and an eye-opener and, as I have said before, if you discover clues to unsolved aspects of the mysterious that we have not stumbled across as you make the same journey then so much the better. Life will indeed be the richer for it. Good hunting.

Beelzebub and The Antrobus Soul Gang

The Feast of All Souls at the beginning of November echoes, under a thin cloak of Christianity, a Celtic festival of the dead for it is the time of the division of the year when winter is heralded. May is the time for re-birth, when the festival of Beltaine was, and still is, held. The most important of these two ceremonies was the heralding of winter, the time we now call Hallowe'en or All Hallows Eve, a time most of us have now given over to the witches, demons and boggarts or buggins. But in the heartland of rural Cheshire a custom still exists at this turning point of the year that has its origins in pagan Celtic tradition and beyond. It has been passed down from father to son and uncle to nephew as the years have come and gone and as far as anyone is aware it is a tradition that has, almost, never been halted.

The Antrobus Soulers have performed their ritual since the mists of time were first formed and even the evil of Adolph Hitler could not stop this festival of fertility, fortune and faith taking place for when the male participants were fighting the foe during the second world war their young sons and young nephews carried on this tradition until they returned from the battlefields.

Opposite page: Beelzebub, complete with frying pan and phallic nose. One of the Antrobus Soulers.

At the time of All Souls in 1993 I and Hilary, my wife, received the great honour of being allowed to accompany the Antrobus Soulers, or the Antrobus "Gang" as they prefer to be called, on their journey round the Cheshire lanes visiting hostelries where they gave their performance and we were given a rare insight into what these fine folk are all about. Outsiders are more than welcome to watch, and to some degree participate, as the Play unfolds in the pubs around Antrobus village but the enactment of the ritual is something more than an entertaining diversion, it is a performance that must take place to ensure the well-being of the good people of Antrobus, especially the Soulers and their families.

Just before the men set out on their nightly journey to act

out their performance, we chatted together. I must admit that, at first, they were a little wary about this writer and his missus coming into their midst and wishing to accompany them on their journey. Perhaps they thought we would be millstones around their necks, or perhaps they thought we would not understand what they are all about and would write fanciful prose about this "quaint" country ritual. However, a pint or two of beer and a discussion about the aesthetic aspects of their forthcoming task turned them round and, when the time came for us to part company they were handing out genuine invitations for us to return again. We shall gladly take them up on this.

During our chat before they set off on their meanderings for that particular night I did not need to ask any of them why they were doing it. It was obvious to them and, if I was to share their hospitality and be privy to their actions and thoughts them it should be obvious to me (and Hilary). However, one of them took it upon himself to explain that some people "knock on wood" to ensure luck and they feel they must do it in a certain way; perhaps with two or maybe three fingers and the knocking has to be a certain rhythm otherwise the benefit is not forthcoming. It is the same with the Soulers. If their tradition is not enacted in a certain way at a certain time then all will not be well. The men of Antrobus have ensured that all will be well for countless centuries by carrying out their own ritual. Originally good fortune meant fertility for crops, animals and the people themselves. Now it means whatever it is wished to mean.

Mystical Story-teller

On that particular night at the beginning of November, the Gang met at the Antrobus Arms and, as is their custom, only then deciding where they were to travel on that particular outing. As it happened they and we concluded at the Ring o' Bells, Daresbury (famous for its associations with the mystical story-teller and Anglican priest Charles Lutwidge Dodgson, known as Lewis Carroll) before moving back to more familiar territory at the Antrobus Arms.

This rustic drama has been traced in various forms back to Neolithic times. The participants are known throughout Britain under various names including Mummers, Geesers or Geese Dancers, Pace Eggers and White Boys. Some of their rituals take place at Easter, others at Christmas.

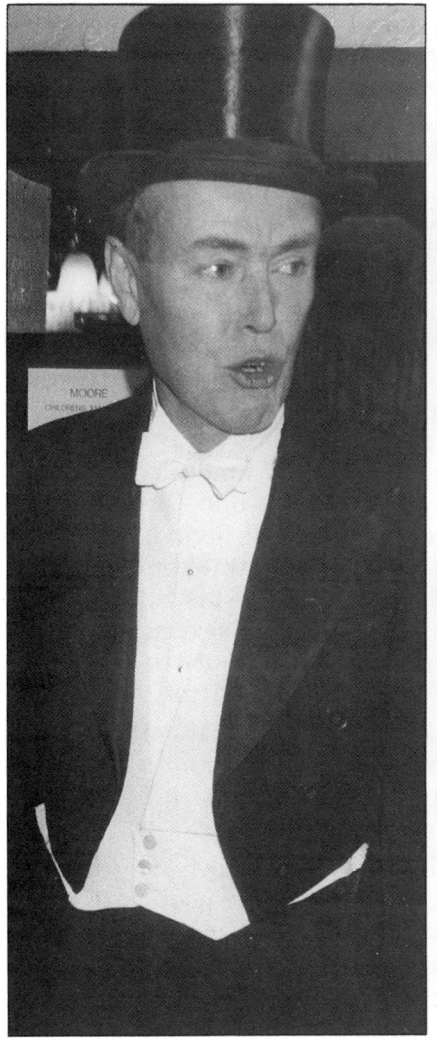

Left: The Letter-In ... was he the inspiration for the Mad Hatter or, perhaps, the White Rabbit? Right: Little Dicky ... perhaps the Wonderland writer was inspired by this character to invent Tweedledum and Tweedledee?

So what about the ancient ritual enacted by the Gang? The first character to enter the chosen public house is the Letter-In, resplendent in a tailcoat, top hat and waistcoat like the character in *Alice in Wonderland*, the White Rabbit. This character opened the tale of the Wonderland adventures and the Letter-In opens the way for the Mummers' tale. Perhaps the famous author witnessed the Soul Gang in the 1800s, who knows? The character could also pass for the Mad Hatter visualised by Dodgson for its top hat and tailcoat are very similar to the attire of the Hatter. He tells the customers at the pub to welcome the "jolly good lads" and to make room for them. There then enters Good King George, in Victorian ceremonial army attire, and then the Black Prince. Whether this Black Prince was supposed to characterise Edward, Prince of Wales (1330-76) or a Saracen Prince from the Crusades it is not now possible to establish, although in some plays in other parts of Britain he is known as the Black Prince of Paradise, the Turkish Prince and Bold Slasher. Perhaps the Black Prince is none other than the Prince of Darkness himself. Anyway, today's character sports a Victorian army tunic and his face and hands are the colour of Cherry Blossom shoe shine. King George and the Prince do battle with swords and the Prince expires on the floor. Along comes Mary, the character traditional of many enactments of life over death, good over evil, spring following winter. This She Male – a man dressed in female garments, but not in a sexual way – has surfaced this century in the pantomime dame but the dual male and female role has long been a part of ancient ritual.

The Man/Woman character can also be seen at Abbotts Bromley in Staffordshire when the annual Horn Dance, another fertility ceremony, is held and "she" can also be seen in *Alice in Wonderland* as the Queen of Hearts, I believe.

That the name of Mary should be given to this Souler is interesting because it has been conjectured by a few people, not least Robert Graves in "The White Goddess" that Robin Hood's Merry Men should be Mary's Men, the followers of the Virgin Mary, the names Mary, Marian and Morris (as in Morris Dancers) being from the same derivation. Morris was originally Maris says Graves, a symbolic name for Mary. The earliest spelling of this name in England, he says, was Marian. So the Morris Dancers and, who knows, perhaps the Mummers and Soulers, were followers of the

Cult of Mary and not necessarily the Virgin Mary but perhaps the Magdalen or Mary of Egypt. Both of these had unusual cultish followings in the Middle Ages. The Maid Marian of Robin Hood fame had a lot to do with the May Queen ceremonials of old ... the contrasting time of year to All Souls.

Mary, the She-Male.

But back to the Antrobus Soul Gang: Mary is in great despair at the demise of the Black Prince, her son, and she calls for the Quack Doctor who enters accompanied by Beelzebub and declares the Black Prince dead. However he revives him with some potions poured down his throat (as Alice takes potions and is revived in Wonderland), including the herb betony or wood betony and in 1935 the Quack Doctor was recorded as saying (*The Country Diary of a Cheshire Man*, Major Arnold Boyd, Collins, 1946) that with the assistance of this herb "if a man has nineteen devils in his heart I can cast twenty one out." The Doctor leaves. The Prince and the King fight again and the Letter-in stops them.

The scene is then set for another character, a pubescent boy, to enter. His name is Little Dicky Derry Doubt, or a similar derivation, and this character, played by a man, is full of sexual innuendo, drawing attention to his lower regions with an over-long tie, two conkers on strings and his shirt tail hanging from his trouser flies, undoubtedly a symbolic character heralding the Spring and May frolics and also a character being menacingly impish. I would here draw your attention to the young Tweedledum and Tweedledee in "Alice" and again wonder whether Lewis Carroll drew inspiration from the Cheshire Soulers.

During this period, there has been lurking the character named Beelzebub, the Prince of Demons and Lord of the Flies. His appendage of Prince of Demons is given in the Bible, Matthew xii. 24, and his appearance at Antrobus (and other places) is something of an enigma. Beelzebub ranked above Satan in the hierarchy of Hell and he was part of Jewish popular belief at the time of Christ. He was Lord of the Flies because he was a creature of decay and corruption and flies are generated in moulding corpses. These corpses were cast into the fires and at Antrobus the character appears to be lurking and awaiting a body to go into the fires of hell, in the form of a frying pan he carries with him, but to no avail. He calls it his Dribble Pan. He settles for drinking the pub customers' ale and never once did I see anyone complain at his downing their pints in one fell swoop. This character may have developed into some form of fertility symbol as well because he sports a huge phallic red nose although this could equally be a remnant of previous ideas of how this character should look.

Enter now the final two characters, the Wild Horse and his Man

Cheshire: its Magic and Mystery

dressed in red hunting garb. We are told that once he, the horse, was alive and now he is dead and all that is left is his head. This hobby horse is essential to the play: onto the floor it drops manure, in the guise of some potatoes, thus ensuring the ground is fertile – although many onlookers do not see the significance of this. At one time nearly every village in this part of the Cheshire heartland performed these ceremonial plays to ward off evil and encourage fertility and good luck and each village jealously guarded their horse head. Indeed, this is still the case today. At one time when there was great rivalry among the villages it was not uncommon for the young bucks from one village to steal the horse head from another and this caused great consternation and public disorder. To this day the horse head is looked after like the Crown Jewels themselves and I noticed that immediately after the public showing of the Antrobus horse the head is carefully wrapped and hidden away. ("Off with his head" shouts the Queen over and over again in the Wonderland book).

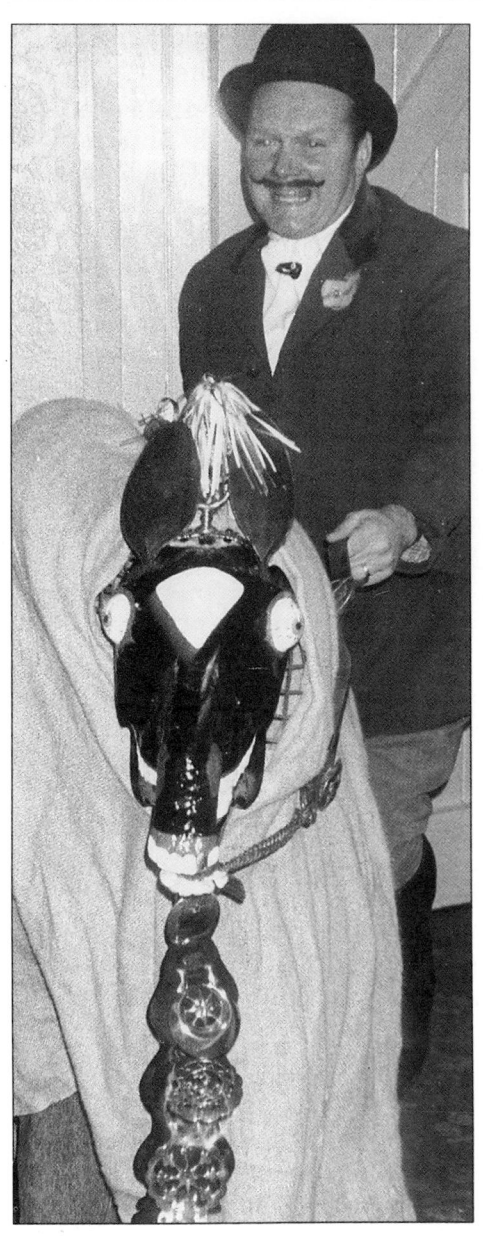

The horse...what the Soulers are all about.

The Antrobus Gang boasted to me of their relatively unbroken line of Soulers. At the nearby village of Comberbach the Comberbach Soulers are enacting the Souling Play as well and I am told they had a comparatively short break but I'm delighted that they can be seen travelling the area at All Souls and breathing new life into their ancient tradition. They use the skull of a real horse and have wired up its jaws so that it snaps open and shut I believe. Perhaps this was how the horse head used to be, who knows? It would certainly connect with the Celtic Cult of the Head and the worship of the horse and skulls. I must admit I detected a friendly rivalry between the two Gangs and it was easy to see how in days now gone this rivalry could have been something other than friendly. But not so now.

In the book by Major Boyd, who lived locally, he referred to the Comberbach Soulers play as almost being a victim of the first world war when the players were away but the youngsters of the village took over. When the men returned the Black Prince sported a German soldier's helmet! This was echoed at Antrobus in the next world war of course when the youngsters held the fort.

Celtic Egg Myth

At one time there were many horse heads belonging to various villages in the keeping of Lord Egerton who displayed them in his Hall. A Celtic myth had the horse as having been created by being hatched from an egg, the symbol of creation, and the Greek fertility goddess Demeter was sometimes represented with the head of a horse – just two examples of the connection of the horse head with birth or fertility. The Antrobus horse can be likened to the hobby horse in the Abbotts Bromley horn dance. The head and snapping jaw and the mane looking like a small tuft and the performer in a cloak or other material are similar to the Oss of Abbotts Bromley – and also the Padstow Obby Oss to some extent.

Both Antrobus and Abbotts Bromley (and Comberbach) can still be proud of their traditions stretching back to pre-Christian times. The enactments possess similar characters and the rituals have been passed on from fathers to sons over the centuries.

This is no co-incidence. It is simply that in these two areas, both rural, there survives tradition that has been handed down for possibly thousands upon thousands of years. This tradition stems from a similar source ... our forebears.

How fortunate we are that these echoes of the past still reverberate in modern society. Now, both village Soulers tend to go around pubs in the area to act their plays but no doubt at one time houses would have been visited to bring good luck. This still occurs at Abbotts Bromley where specific houses are visited, not to mention the local manor house. There are other areas of course that keep the old traditions alive. Padstow in Cornwall has its own Obby Oss and there thousands of people participate in the annual ceremony of fertility and good fortune but here in Cheshire it has, thankfully, not been commercialised.

I have read that Major Boyd, of whom I have previously made mention, helped "to revive" the Soulers although the Gang members I spoke to were all of the opinion that the Antrobus Gang's record was unbroken. Perhaps it referred to the fact that Major Boyd offered his services when there was a shortage of someone to play a role, who knows? He certainly had an affinity with Cheshire and may very well have had something to do with the Soulers and anyone who has read his book will know that not only did he appreciate the natural beauty of this county but he knew of its traditions as well.

At Tarvin there was, certainly into the mid-1920s, a Souling Gang who gave their performance on All Souls Eve but why it stopped I do not know. It went the way of so many in Cheshire around that time when anything of the past was deemed unfashionable. It was the future they looked to then. According to *The Cheshire Village Book* produced by the Cheshire Federation of Women's Institutes the Black Prince there was known as the Cheshire Champion and it gives a verse of the souling song exclusive to Tarvin recorded on paper in 1891 as:

Your lanes they are dirty, and your meadows grow cold,
And if you are willing with us you may go,
We will bring you safe back again, you have no need to fear,
And it's all that we are souling for is your ale and strong beer

At Lymm there is a tradition that "Horse's Head" plays used to be performed around the ancient cross. Presumably these were Soul Plays. This cross, partly built on a natural outcrop of sandstone, has been used long before Christianity. It became a Christian cross sometime around the Norman invasion, I believe, but has been used as the focal point of the community for countless years.

I am told that at Alderley Park, a mansion house now owned by ICI, now Zeneca but previously by the Stanleys, there used to be a Mummers' or Soulers' Play performed at Christmas by the tenants. I suspect this was a Soulers' Play that found its way to Christmas-time for the amusement of the Stanleys who revelled in re-vamped traditions such as the Yule Log being dragged to the Tenants Hall and being lit at the banquet laid on for the estate tenants. This performance of Mumming or Souling was certainly taking place at the turn of the century when Lord and Lady Sheffield, another branch of the Stanley line, were at the Hall. On their deaths it was inherited by their son, Lord Stanley of Alderley. It was at this time that the estate was sold at auction and many tenants purchased their own properties. The Mummers or Soulers ceased at this period.

In Barthomley, at the very heart of rural Cheshire, the Soulers are recorded as having been youngsters. In 1856, a Vicar the Rev. Edward Hinchcliffe, M.A., who had been in charge of the souls of Barthomley for 14 years until 1850 (and who was born and bred in the village) wrote a book called "Barthomley." Several customs are described including Souling on All-Souls Eve. He wrote: "This sweet melody of music, for many years of my life, often reached me when I had retired to rest, and its plaintive tones, softened by distance, used to lull me gradually to sleep. The song of the children was short and to the point:

> *"Soul, soul, for an apple or two,*
> *If you have no apples, pears will do;*
> *Pray, good mistress, a soul cake."*

Barthomley is a village that still retains the magic that once abounded in Cheshire. It is one of the spiritual parts of the county's whole and there is much more to tell within this book of this entrancing, enchanting and spiritual place. And there is much still to discover.

Cheshire has, like other counties, lost many of its traditions but it is fighting to hang on to what it still has, thank goodness. And it has plenty. There is no doubt in my mind that the Soulers will continue to travel the lanes of Cheshire and re-enact a tradition that is older than the county itself. It is in their blood. It is in their souls.

2

Worshipping the trees

Across the Palatine throughout the ages people have looked upon the thorn tree – and other trees and bushes – as sacred. Of course most of this veneration took place in days long gone but it would be a mistake to assume it does not happen today, for it does. How many of us have used the phrase "Knock on wood" for instance? All we are doing is invoking old thoughts of a spirit whose abode was a tree. At the village of Appleton, now known as Appleton Thorn, local children still dance around a thorn tree after it has been bedecked with garlands and at Over Alderley on the Congleton to Alderley Road there stands the remains of a stone cross that was, earlier this century, overgrown by a thorn tree long looked upon with awe by the local folk.

It is not just the thorn tree that was, and is, thought of as special. The oak and the elder play a role, as does the yew tree, especially those ancient yews planted on the sites of churches before churches themselves were planted. And some people still visit trees because those trees possess, it is believed, healing properties.

There are many more instances. The ancient oak tree at Marton, referred to as the "Marton Oak", has long been protected not only because of its size and age but because of the respect for the healing properties of its bark. At Mottram St Andrew near to the site of a moated medieval building once known as Foxtwist Hall there is a tree visited for its so-called healing values. And the village of Alderley derives its name from the mystical Alder or Eller tree, revered by our predecessors as a symbol of the gods and, therefore, something to be worshipped.

Trees hold a magic all their own. This curious tree used to be in Byrons Wood, Macclesfield, and was looked upon as something special in Victorian times.

Children up until this century would dance around the Alder tree and recite rhymes, often meaningless to them but let us return to the thorn tree, the hawthorn or May Thorn, of which the old adage "Don't cast a clout 'til May be out" refers. Many Thorn trees, because of the fact that they were something special – perhaps said to have been planted by a holy person or were thought to be the abode of a tree spirit or were used to mark the scene of a battle or the grave of a venerated being – became marking points or boundary markers. A good example of this is at Three Shire Heads on the Cheshire border with Staffordshire and Derbyshire where there is an area known as Cut Thorn, undoubtedly the thorn tree with cuts or marks on it being used to designate the boundary of three Shires.

Bawming the Thorn

A thorn tree at Appleton Thorn is of particular interest because here tree worship still goes on, albeit now in a Christianised form.

Around midsummer children from the local primary school parade to the spot and dance around the thorn tree situated outside the church and across the road from the Thorn public house. This tree is bedecked with garlands and bright ribbons and decorated with flowers and today these local school children participants sing verses written only a century or so ago as they dance and skip around the tree and hold their arms aloft as though in an act of worship. Local tradition has it that in 1178 the Lord of the Manor by the name of Adam de Dutton brought to the village a thorn tree said to have been an offshoot of the Glastonbury Thorn – the remarkable tree that grew, it is said, from Joseph of Arimathea's staff planted in the ground at Glastonbury. It flowered at Christmas and later when the Gregorian calendar came into use it became early January. Adam was also responsible for setting up the stone cross at Appleton, it is claimed. He took part in the Crusades and the bringing of the thorn tree and erecting the cross are acts supposed to be in thanks for his safe return.

I think otherwise. My belief is that the people of Appleton, in days when Christianity was struggling to be the dominant religion, worshipped their own gods, albeit pagan or non-Christian. This was not uncommon, it happened throughout the length and breadth of the British Isles, and this particular worship was at sites special to the particular area. Whether or not at Appleton it took the form of worshipping a sacred tree can only be surmised but I would say it is extremely likely. On to the scene came the obviously pious Adam, fresh from his Crusade, who replaced the pagan tree with a Christianised one, this being a supposed offshoot of Britain's own Christian tree, the Glastonbury Thorn. Where the Appleton Thorn now stands, protected by iron railings, there was I believe this earlier sacred tree. The traditional dancing around and adorning of a tree was allowed to continue but with the eye of the Church cast over proceedings, as it is today. What we see now was revived only in 1973 and had ceased in 1933.

Schoolchildren pay homage to the sacred tree ... Bawming the Thorn at Appleton Thorn.

The Appleton thorn bedecked with garlands.

The Church stands just by the ceremonial site, no doubt originally built at a pagan place, and going by the unusual name of St Cross. Could this name refer to a Sanctified Cross – a pagan stone or cross that Adam did not in fact erect but made Christian or sanctified? It could very possibly have been a stone monolith that marked this site of special significance.

The ceremony we witness today is but an imitation of that once held but perhaps in-born memories still linger and the children raising their arms to the tree and dancing around it echo visions of the past in one form or another. Certainly the act of bedecking trees was not unusual up until the twentieth century but it is now all but lost. At Clun in Shropshire a form of tree dressing still occurs but the Bawming the Thorn ceremony at Appleton is undoubtedly the last ceremony of its kind in these isles. But what about the word "Bawm", pronounced "Borm", itself? Interestingly the German and Saxon for tree is "baum" and "balm" is a healing substance from a tree. In the Appleton context it is used to describe the act of adorning the tree – perhaps in an effort to heal or preserve life as in embalm or embaum.

In days long before the Norman Conquest, thorn trees were the supposed dwelling places of gods and they could not be cut or damaged in any way for the wrath of that particular tree resident would rain down on the culprit. As far back as the Celts, who rejoiced in the Sacred Groves in the forested lands of Britain, the thorn bush or tree was special. The Celtic Bards had a ceremony at which they encircled a thorn tree and offered it branches from other sacred trees.

Not so very far away from Appleton and very much in Cheshire is the hamlet of Nether Alderley straddling the trunk road from Congleton. By the side of this road at the crossing of minor roads there stands the remains of a stone cross or pillar and this has definite associations with a venerated thorn tree. According to an excellent book entitled *Trees of the British Isles in History and Legend* by J.H. Willis (Frederick Muller 1972) this cross was at one time shrouded by a thorn bush. I have in my possession a photograph taken about 1903 which does show this and there is an illustration in *East Cheshire* written by I.P. Earwaker in the nineteenth century depicting the cross covered over by a tree or bush.

A rare old photograph from my collection of the thorn tree on top of the remains of the stone cross known as Alderley Cross.

J.H. Willis states that a local history of 1903 says : "The cross is embraced with a thorn tree that is probably the Glastonbury Thorn of the Stanley memoirs and a successor to the staff of Joseph of Arimathea." The Stanleys, whose stately home at Alderley Park is now owned by ICI (now called Zeneca), were devout church people and I would suggest that, just as at Appleton, the cutting of the Glastonbury Thorn was imported to replace something pagan or non Christian. The stone cross or stone pillar was obviously placed there because of the site's special importance. The Stanleys came on the scene around the 1500s and the "cross" is certainly older than that so perhaps here we have an instance of the Christian

Thorn Tree replacing a pagan stone or maybe there was another thorn tree growing over the stone before the Stanleys came and it replaced that.

Healing Oak

A few miles in a southerly direction is the village of Marton that boasts the oldest black and white church still in use in Europe and where there is a stone pillar in the church grounds. Just a little way away across the main road is Oak Lane. Travel down there and in the private grounds of a house by Oak Farm there stands the famous Marton Oak. It did used to be on land owned by Oak Farm and was used as a tethering place for a bull, but is now in the possession of the adjacent property's owners. If you should wish to view this oak I must emphasise it is – at the time of writing – on private land and permission must be sought. This tree is now split into three parts and was at one time said to be the largest oak in the entire country. At its base its girth was 58 feet and the largest of its branches was 11 feet six inches around. Today a small wooden play house has been erected at the base. This ancient tree of unknown age has, not surprisingly, been looked upon as something special and I was told by a resident of the village in the 1970s that a small piece of its bark would be used for ridding the body of warts, rashes and boils, by rubbing the bark on afflicted parts. A piece of the bark used to be placed in nearby farms and cottages to ward away the "evil eye". There was, at one time, a similar tree at Siddington that gave its name to Broad Oak Farm but it is, alas, no more.

Throughout this country many oak trees are venerated and many tales are told of them. They were used as preaching sites – although there is no evidence of this having taken place at Marton – and they were used as meeting places for the community although, again, there is no evidence of this at Marton. But what there is evidence of is the plain fact that this tree has been preserved with much love and affection over the years with its branches and trunks being propped up and it receiving an annual "manicure" up until recent times when its branches were carefully lopped on a regular basis.

The healing oak ... the famous and ancient Marton Oak from an old photograph. Today it is on private property.

The late Dr Stella Davies, in her book *Agricultural History of Cheshire* (Chetham Society, 1960), gives a brief and intriguing quotation from a notice which was circularized to the tenants of Henry Tomkinson at Bunbury in 1815. It said: "Any person lopping oak trees for the ridiculous custom of decorating houses on May 29th will be prosecuted under the recent Act which allows transportation for life for such an offence". I rather fancy Lord and Master Tomkinson was a bit over the top regarding transportation for life for lopping a tree but his outburst gives an insight into the custom of Oak Apple Day on May 29th – the day of the restoration of Charles II to the English throne in 1660. (Bunbury is discussed elsewhere in this book; it is a village that epitomises the Cheshire Earth Spirit. Much of its magic has been retained; I would recommend a visit to those who have not sampled its spiritual delight).

Oak Apple Day was sometimes known as Royal Oak Day or Oakleaf Day. At schools throughout Cheshire, woe betide anyone who was not sporting an oak leaf on that day or the other children would nettle their legs or perform some other mischievous act. Here, pupils of Bollington Central School wear oak leaves on May 29th, 1930.

Oak leaves and oak apples were worn in memory of the King who took refuge in an oak tree while hiding from his pursuers, hence the Royal Oak pub signs. "Oak Leaf Day" or "Oak Apple Day" was celebrated throughout Cheshire by the wearing of oak leaves and it was extremely common up until the middle of this century when it died a natural death. Very few places and very few people still celebrate this day. It was, I think, a remnant of something much older than the time of King Charles. It has its roots set firmly in the Druidic traditions and the Celtic customs of tree worship and the veneration of the oak tree. It was allowed to be retained, or resurrected, in celebration of the defeat of Puritanism.

The oak seems to attract lightning far more than any other species. The Lightning Oak had associations with the Thunder God and any such oak struck by lightning was, and is, special. People would journey for miles to take a piece from such a tree and wear it as a talisman for luck and protection. One Druid chant to the sacred oak has come down to us today as "Hip, Hip Hooray" and likewise was the odd phrase "Hey Nonny No".

Tarry for a while if you can at a spot thought by many to be one of the few remaining Sacred Groves. It is at a tiny corner of Cheshire known as Fools Nook or, correctly, Oak Grove. It lies just south of Macclesfield on the main road to Leek and although little is left of this magical and mysterious spot there are enough trees (and a fine hostelry) to make a detour worthwhile. I discuss this interesting and intriguing spot in a previous book *Magic, Myth and Memory* and must not repeat it here, but suffice to say this is where the "Fools" or those who were not Christian (the Celts) had their shrine or church – in the Oak Grove. There is now a sadness about this place; it has been ruined by man and there is also a sense of foreboding around there; my apologies to its residents but I feel they know what I am hinting at.

Wild Floralia

In the Merry Month of May there is a time still recognised as Beltaine, sacred to the Bards and Druids of the Celts who worshipped the oak. It is on May Day, the time for dancing around a tree or wooden phallus, that ceremonies were held to induce fertility. The time of May Day or Beltaine when the may tree or may pole is worshipped was not liked by pious Christians of old. The very fact that it was a blatantly sexual ceremony did not stand it in good stead and much suppression took place. However, the Church later allowed tradition to hang on by encouraging the dancing around the pole but discouraging the frolics that went with it; and now there is little or no indication of the goings on of old for it is toned down to become, for instance, an attraction at a village fete, a pleasant diversion between the running of the three legged race and the cream buns being served. At Rostherne Church, for example, close by the magical mere, there is the grave of a fiery Puritan minister who actively discouraged locals going a-Maying. The Reverend Adam Martindale, who died at neighbouring High Legh in 1686, had strong words to say about the May ritual. Mr Martindale had his opponents in the parish and on one occasion people – to whom he referred to as "The rabble of profane youths and some doting fools" – sought to annoy him by erecting a maypole on the path he took from the vicarage to the church.

He is recorded as having said of this: "I took an effectual way to rout them. I preached at them, telling them that a maypole was a a relic of the shameful worship of the strumpet Flora in Rome." He got a visiting preacher, Mr Brooke of Congleton, to talk on the subject and he "did most smartly reprove their sin and folly, calling them scum, rabble and riff-raff of the parish." Mr Martindale's wife went further than either and with the assistance of three ladies of the parish "whipt the maypole down in the night with a framing saw, cutting it breast high, so as the bottom would serve well for a diall post."

The May ceremonies were indeed, as the preacher said, associated with the Roman goddess of Spring, Flora. Their festival has been described as "rather wild" and was named the Floralia.

How different from the tame and ineffectual ceremonies of dancing around the maypole enacted today at village fetes and at schools, watched over by the church. How many who take part in the maypole dances realise that the may pole was once a May Tree and the phallic symbol was worshipped to ensure fertility for man, woman, animals and crops? The Bawming the Thorn ceremony was very much in this tradition. It has all now been "watered down" to suit our modern society.

Many trees have been venerated for the power that people can get from them and have been used for healing purposes. Here is one that used to be known as a healing tree at Mottram St Andrew.

In the centre of the village of Eaton near to Tarporley there used to stand a stone pillar or cross and it must be presumed that this was demolished as part of the Puritan zeal that took over the country a few centuries ago although a new one was erected to celebrate the Queen's Jubilee. Indeed, most stone pillars in our county were toppled over by these Puritans; their bases can still be seen at spots such as churchyards and a number of the pillars have been utilised as sun dials. However, the site of this cross used to contain a hawthorn tree and it used to be the venue for the May Day celebrations. It is common knowledge that this tree was planted there in the 1800s but I wonder whether this was, in fact, re-planted. Perhaps the old tree died and another took its place or perhaps it was a folk memory of what used to be. We look in greater detail at these May-time customs of Cheshire elsewhere in this book but Eaton was also a great place for Souling and this was carried out chiefly by the children who went from house to house in a quest for pennies. Their parents seemed to be content with "ale, gin or brandy" according to the Eaton Souling Song I once had the pleasure of listening to, courtesy of a fine old Eatonite by the name of William.

Many Cheshire churchyards have yew trees within them and the majority of them are very old indeed. But perhaps the oldest is at Astbury near Congleton where local tradition has it that it is over one thousand years old and is older than the church itself. This could show that there was a yew tree there before a Christian church was built upon the site and, perhaps, this was the site of a Druid Grove. The yew featured prominently in Celtic belief.

There is both yew and oak growing at the site of the Holy Well at Alderley Edge, an obvious Sacred Grove if ever there was one. The chapter on Sacred Waters looks at this more fully.

Perhaps we should look at our Cheshire trees with different eyes, for many have had the power to heal and many could still retain this power.

The ancient yew at Astbury. It is in all probability older than the church itself and points to there having been at one time a Celtic holy place at the site. This tree could well be a descendant of an original yew planted by Druids or Ovates long before Christianity.

Taken in 1905 the picture shows damage caused by a burst water pipe on the Lake Vyrnwy to Liverpool pipe track that was laid in 1886. The site stands on the meeting place of five roads and the cross has been described as both a preaching cross and market cross. The hawthorn was planted by James Platt (1829-94) of Oak Tree Farm. Tradition has it that the cross was not destroyed by Puritans but was hidden by villagers. I wonder if it is on land at Oak Tree Farm?

Cheshire: its Magic and Mystery

A rare photograph showing a tree growing from the cross at Eaton near Chester given to me by John Ennion of Beeston Moss.

Another view of the tree at Eaton. J.Ennion.

3

A-Maying in The Land of The Green Man

All on this pleasant morning together we will go
For summer springs so fresh, green and gay
We'll tell you of a blossom here that hangs on every bough
Drawing near is the merry month of May.
Rise up the young man of this house, put on your coat of blue,
And to the girl that you love best, we hope you will be true;
Drawing near is the merry month of May.
So now we're going to leave you in peace and plenty here
For summer springs so fresh and green and gay
And we'll come no more a-May singing until another year
For to drive cold winter away.

This is one of several traditional Cheshire May Songs – with other verses – and has been preserved thanks to Beatrice Tunstall in her book *The Shiny Night* (William Heinemann 1931) and also thanks to Robert Holland of Mobberley, a relation of Knutsford's Mrs Gaskell, when he penned an introduction to the book *Flora of Cheshire* by Lord de Tabley. These songs or chants were performed by groups of people, usually young, who went from door to door in the same way as we today go a-carolling at Yuletide. It was as common up until the first world war as carol singing is today and vied with the Cheshire Soul Gangs for popularity. May was a time for merrymaking in the merry month; it was also a time for fornication and frolic, for fun, friendship and frivolity. It was the time to welcome in the sun and it was the time to forget the rigours of winter. It was a time when there was every excuse for not only letting off steam but for generally having a damn good time.

This was the time when youngsters could dance around a symbolic giant phallus and get away with it; it was a time when sexual innuendo and mischief was excusable. It was a time when everyone expected everyone else to do just that.

Celebrating the May ... Morris Men at Knutsford Royal May Day processing just as their predecessors would have done for centuries except the musical instruments may well have been a fife and drum or fiddle in the past. How different the Morris Men's performance sounds with what I term the "real" musical instruments compared with those used today.

It is no surprise that the May month was Cheshire's pride; the county that relies so much on agriculture and the bounty of the earth should, after all, celebrate the time when farm animals get together to produce their offspring and the time when seeds of every variety are sown. This was, and is, the time of sowing in order to reap. It is the time when the symbols of fertility – Jack in the Green, the Green Man and the Man of the Greenwood (Robin the Good Fellow) should have an airing.

The Spirit of the Man in Green and his Merrymaking Men still roam the plains and the peaks of our Cestrian landscape; his heart still beats in the landscape; his sap still rises in the green wood and he still worships the Mother Goddess Mary-on (Marion). Can it really be any wonder that the most famous of ballads depicting Robin Hood was dedicated to the Earl of Chester? This is as much the haunt of Robin of the Hood as is Nottinghamshire. That county has commercialised its claim to the Earth Spirit but Cheshire folk have been in awe of the same Puckish sprite for as many centuries.

There have been many attempts to stop these customs. The traditions stem back to Celtic and, indeed, pre-Celtic periods and so these attempts have, in the main, proved to be futile. The genes of a thousand ancestors still linger in the make-up of a Cestrian and cannot easily be vanquished. The strongest attempt to sweep these "nasty" and impure frolics under the carpet was made by the Puritans but that failed. There is a document (Chetham Society O.S. Vol 3) that tells of the Vicar of Rostherne, a Puritan, who put a stop to a-Maying. However, he wrote in his autobiography that at the Restoration he was kicked out by the locals (or deprived of his Living). "The rabble of prophane youths and some doting fooles that tooke their parte, were encouraged to affront me, by setting up a Maypole in my way to the church." he wrote. This gentleman, obviously extremely sincere in his beliefs, thought it best to ignore this phallus and let them get on with their shouting and abuse. He waited for the fun and games to die down and began to preach a sermon to the crowd "How long, ye simple men, will you love simplicity?", taken from Proverbs 1. 22.

Washington Irving wrote that by the banks of the Dee at Chester "close by pictureque old bridge that stretches across the river" he saw a Maypole and he imagined the sight of people "with all the dancing revelry of May-day". Here I must thank Joan Leach for her extremely well-documented *History of Knutsford Royal May Day* and she mentions there are two maypoles marked on a Chester map of 1745; she says these were the focal points for a rowdy Jacobite demonstration during the year 1712 when cart-loads of people went from the pole outside the North Gate to the pole at Handbridge playing "When the King in joy his owne again". Perhaps the one seen by Washington Irving made a third or perhaps it was the one at Handbridge he was referring to. There is mention, also, in Christina Hoyle's *Folklore of Cheshire.*

There are other instances in Cheshire of the May Pole being a permanent construction. I have heard an oral tradition of one being constructed by the Crosses at Sandbach; there was most certainly one at Alderley and Bunbury had one some many hundreds of years ago, it is said.

May Day was also the time to be married. Not surprising, really, for the Cheshire people looked upon this as the celebration of fertility and so what better time could there be for a young couple? You will notice in the A-Maying song that young lads are urged to put on their coat of blue and another verse tells the girl to put on her gown of silk. This was so they could perform the rituals to become married ... not necessarily in the eyes of the church. This was the time that was also known as Wedding Day; and in many Cheshire villages on Wedding Day the ground would be decorated with grains of different coloured sands. It is thought this was to wish upon them as many children as grains of sand, yet another ritual to invoke fertility. This tradition remains in Knutsford on the day of the town's May Day celebrations. Unfortunately now it is not always possible for the May Day celebrations to be on May Day itself but is on the nearest Saturday to it. At Knutsford local tradition places this sanding ritual with King Canute. The popular belief now is that the town was so named because of Canute's Ford as King Canute is supposed to have crossed the river and, pausing to let sand fall out of his shoes, saw a couple who were to be married and he wished them as many children as grains of sand. This is a good indication of how traditions bend to the locality for, having claimed Canute as the town's name-giver they claim him as ritual-maker as well. This custom has almost died out in the rest of the county but, thank goodness, Knutsford retains it and long may it be so. Knutsford folk can now, also, claim their tradition as being "unique" by virtue of it dying out everywhere else. And as for the naming of the town after Canute crossing one of the two rivers there? Well, maybe. It is quite possible that the King did indeed cross a river there, but he must have crossed rivers over the length and breadth of the land. Perhaps he, or his army, controlled a strategic crossing there. We are never going to know for sure and I wish "Royal" Knutsford well in retaining not only the tradition of Canute but the Sanding as well.

If anyone wishes to see this in action then visit Knutsford on the morning of the May Day procession and the pavements outside several pubs are sanded, as are a number of other spots including outside the Parish Church. I must say, however, that on recent visits I have been saddened to see visitors walking over the Sandings and thereby destroying them. Not so very long ago the crowds of spectators would have carefully avoided this act of desecration but now, it seems, alas, no.

Knutsford can also claim its own fertility symbol in Jack in the Green who proudly leads the May Day parade. We shall be looking at Jack o' Knutsford and more Green Men of Cheshire a little later

May Day in Cheshire was the time when the May Birchers went their rounds and it was a time dreaded by many people. For this was the time when branches torn off trees were placed above doors and on house chimneys and those villagers who enacted this ritual, the May Birchers, could be very nasty indeed. They placed branches from trees and shrubs whose names rhymed, supposedly, with characteristics supposed to be typical of the householders.

Beatrice Tunstall's book is a novel, but includes part fact among the fiction, and is set in Cheshire. She tells of the Birchers going to the home of the hero and placing lime there, to say he was "prime" and also broom to add that he was to become a groom. She continued that pear was placed at the farm of his intended to indicate that not only was the bride to be fair but so was the feeling towards the marriage by their neighbours. At the abode of a glum person was delivered plum and alder (in dialect, 'owler') to rhyme with scowler.

Knutsford's famous Mrs Gaskell wrote a letter to her literary editors in 1838 and in it she described this custom taking place at Knutsford. Here, an oak described a good woman (in this case, not in rhyme but her being as solid, in the spiritual sense, as an oak) and a broom was a good housewife. Mrs Gaskell wrote that gorse, nettles, sycamore or sawdust "cast the worst imputation on a woman's character." She added that one of her servant girls had told her that many a poor girl had her character blasted by one of these branches or bushes being hung up by someone who owned her a grudge. This was one of those times when most people wanted to believe there was no smoke without fire.

Bonfires on White Nancy hillside at Kerridge were the order on great occasions stretching back over hundreds and hundreds of years.

The Goodly Fires

It was not only the Pole that was worshipped at May Day. It was also the time of the Beltaine Fires.

This was the celebration of the Druids, those Celtic Shaman or Holy Men, the Learned Ones, who handed down their secrets from father to son ... just like the Cheshire Soul Gangs. There was no written tradition, it was a tradition written only in memories and in genes. May Day was when the bil-tene or goodly fire was lit. It was the time when the fire of Baal was lit and the flames were sent down hills, the Tan or Tarn Hills of Cheshire. Its name can be written in many ways from Beltain to Beal-tine, Beltan, Baltein or Bel-tein. The Eve of this day was the time when dragons fought each other and put people in terror, when babies had to be kept in because demons would steal them and when the doors to fairyland would open. To the ancients, May Day was Calan Mai.

Fires were lit at the turn of all four seasons, in fact, and these Bale Fires marked the progress of the sun in the skies and it was not only the Celts of Cheshire (and other parts) who followed this ritual. Bal or Bel was a god of the ancient Hebrews as well, and Beltaine coincides with the Jewish, and Christian, Pentecost. Fire worship has long been the part of the heritage of the human race and, as I mention in at least two of my previous works, by creating fire here on earth we have been able to re-create the all-giving god, known as Sol, the Sun. Or so our predecessors thought.

Our fair county is not blessed with an absolute abundance of hills; our gardens and farmland were once the flat seabed, a bay in fact, and the waters lapped upon the cliffsides that are now the Pennine ridges around Macclesfield and Congleton and The Edge. It is now from these cliffs, in the main, that the traditions of these Beltaine Fires linger, though there are a number of places – most particularly where the great castle at Beeston was constructed and the surrounding hills of Peckforton – that have been lit by these fires of old also.

In the year 1600, Cheshire's hills were described by one William Smith as: "The country, albeit be in most places flat and even, yet hath int certain Hills of Name (besides the Mountains which divide it from Stafford-shire and Derby-shire) as Frodshum Hills, Peckfarton Hills, Buckley Hills, Helsby Tor, Winecader Hill, Shutlingshlow Hill, Penket Cloud, Congleton Hedge (or Edge), Mowcop Hill, which is a mile, from the foot, to the top, but standeth most part in Stafford-shire."

Undoubtedly the scene of many a goodley fire ... the high hill at Beeston that was used by the Normans and by the pre-Normans as a fortress and by others for the lighting of Beltaine Fires. This is a fanciful idea of how the Castle used to look. J. Ennion.

These fires were formerly kindled with great ceremony and, said J.G. Frazer in *The Golden Bough* the traces of human sacrifices at them were particularly clear and unequivocal. Later, animals were driven through these fires to "cleanse" them and I have been told that this was still going on in certain areas around Nantwich in the 1970s. It could very well be continuing to this day. Although, in the main, these fires were lit on hills they were also lit on the Cheshire plain as well (as the Nantwich case shows) where the Celtic traditions survived. Belief does not require a hill, it requires man's fertile brain and nothing more.

The custom of lighting these fires, according to J.G. Frazer, lasted well into the eighteenth century, but he obviously was not referring to Cheshire and surrounding areas, where it has survived for a great deal longer. Just over the border of Cheshire (although at one time the area was certainly a part of Cheshire) at a rocky outcrop known as The Roaches I have been shown traces of charcoal at a group of boulders called The Ballstones (Stones of Bal?) This could very well have been from some form of ritual fire-lighting that took place this century; and that spot was once in the Forest of Lyme – the area that divided the County Palatine of Cheshire from the rest of the country. I have also been told of the tradition of rolling barrels of tar down the hillside at Kerridge on top of which there stands the folly known as White Nancy. This was performed just beyond living memory – I would say about the late 1870s or 1880s. It was while I and Hilary were living in Chancery Lane in Bollington in the late 1960s and were known to frequent a local hostelry called the Red Lion that this tale unfolded. The landlord and landlady at the time were Flo and Alan Gilbert and they kept a traditional village pub; it was a place where everyone knew everyone – the beer was good and so was the company. Anyway, one of the locals was an elderly gentleman of indeterminate years who lived on his own in Lord Street, just down the way from the Red Lion. He went by the title "Old Joe" and I would say he was certainly in his eighties when he passed on. I remember him as having a wicked eye for the young ladies and he was rather prone to bursting into song: a tune that no-one else could recognise but he entitled it "The Wibbly Wobbly Way". Old Joe told me that he could remember the young lads rolling flaming barrels of tar down the Kerridge hillside. He did not know why and he was at the time too young to participate, so this would make it the late 1870s or the 1880s – I know not exactly. Unfortunately he did not know the time of year; I have not been able to find any record of this and I have never heard of anyone else recalling this so perhaps the "purist" historians will be loathe to accept this. However, I must say that he had no reason whatsoever to make it up and he had no reason at all for bringing it up in conversation with me; it was just a matter of fact as far as he was concerned. I am a firm believer in folk tradition and folk tradition was, in the main, passed on by word of mouth. Just as Old Joe had done to me.

And the hill to which he referred is something more than the site of a folly shaped like a sugar-loaf and the (possible) site of the Beltane Fires – its is undoubtedly a "mammary hill".

Let me explain. Our forefathers of old, before the Celtic tribes were dominant in this land, believed that the earth was a living being and this living being was a mother – Mother Earth. She was the person from whom we all emerged it was thought, and from whom the grass, the trees, the birds and the animals emerged also. This all-giving goddess later became Bridget or Brighit, the Earth Mother (her name is remembered in The Bridestones just inside the Cheshire border near to Bosley Cloud and where people used to go to be married "over the brush" or by passing between the stones). She later became Christianised as Mary and she became associated with the fertility cult of the Green Man, especially around May Day in the form of the Maid, or Virgin, Marian or Marion, a derivation of Mary. There were certain natural formations that, therefore, became places to be held in awe because they resembled part of the female anatomy. The area known as Gradbach in the Cheshire hills above Macclesfield has a stream that flows a browny red and Gradbach used to be known as Great Bitch – the large female. It was quite likely that those of old looked upon these waters flowing red as The Great Bitch menstruating. And at Kerridge the hill looks, when viewed from a number of angles, like the breast of a female. Where the folly called White Nancy is now situated is the spot where the nipple of the breast would be.

Tradition has it that "White Nancy" is so called because it is a corruption of White Ordnance and this may very well be so. It may also derive its name from the white horse that carted the stone to the top of the hill, as another tradition has it; but I wonder whether White Nancy refers to the milky breast of the Earth Mother. It was the Gaskell family who erected the structure on top of the hill, but they erected it not at the very peak but at one side. They erected it, I believe, where there had been a previous structure. This structure was originally to show the nipple of the Mother and it later, I believe, was utilised as a beacon – one of the chain across the length and breadth of this land used to signal anything of importance (there are many in Cheshire, or have been many. Beacon Point at Alderley Edge is but one and the Wirral hills contain several). Toot Hill, above Macclesfield Forest, would most certainly have been used for either look-out purposes or the Goodly Fires; if not both.

A breast of the Earth Mother ... White Nancy Hill again.

Over at Derbyshire there is a hillside known as Mam Tor. This gets its name from being the breast, or mammary, of the Earth Mother.

The rocky crag at Beeston was a beacon point, and still is. I am also of the belief that, long before there was a castle constructed on top of the hill at Beeston this area was one that was held in awe. This rocky hill can be seen from all sections of Cheshire, and is, beyond doubt, the centre of a number of strong earth energy lines. This place of the dragon has been used for ritual purposes since man could walk on two legs. It is no wonder it was chosen as a site for a defensive castle but it is equally no wonder it was chosen for the Goodly Fires. The May Day skies would have been illuminated with flames from on top of Beeston for countless years (and has often, even in these modern times, been used for beacon fires). Later these sacrificial fires would have been rolled down the hill (as some still roll eggs at Easter) and, in all probability, sacrificial victims would have been rolled down the hill at some point in our history as well. The fires would have been witnessed from many points all around the county by awe-inspired beings. It would not have needed too much of a clear day but what a dramatic sight this must have been – like a volcano erupting or the earth spewing out its energies.

I wonder whether Beeston derives its name from these fires?

The prefix "Bee" could, possibly, be derived from Beal or could be derived from the same source as "Beacon". Local legend has it that one midnight countless years ago Satan was flying over Cheshire and had his apron full of stones and one of his apron strings broke and a giant stone fell to earth. This was the crag now known as Beeston.

The Beltaine custom around May Day is firmly set in the Celtic beliefs and one of the foremost experts on Celtic traditions, Ann Ross, has no hesitation in placing the Bog Man discovered at Lindow Common, close by Wilmslow, well and truly into the Beltaine tradition – and who am I to disagree?

She is, in my view, one of the world's top authorities on anything Celtic and her informative study of the Bog Man who was dug out of the peat at the Black Pool at Lindow ranks as a piece of investigation Sherlock Holmes would have been proud of. We look at this in greater detail elsewhere.

Where's Jack?

Traditions of a-Maying, the Beltaine Fires, the May Birchers, Sanding, and the May Pole all have their roots in fertility. Whether it was to ensure the coupling of people or animals or the abundance of crops this is the time of year when rituals had to be enacted. If they were not, then perhaps the continuation and the well-being of the community would be in jeopardy.

Here in lush, fertile, Cheshire it hardly seems necessary to ritually entice crops to grow or cows to give milk. But, for the same reason as the Cheshire Soulers still enact their annual ritual, it is (or was) not so much a case of what would happen if the ceremonies did not take place but of "being on the safe side". What, after all, was the point in not doing something that was not only a bit of fun but had a serious purpose as well?

It is from these traditions that another memory of that which has passed still survives. The spirit of the Green Man.

And survive he most certainly does. He is kept alive at the May Day Festival at Knutsford, he is kept alive in many Cheshire churches in carvings sometimes referred to as foliate heads and he is kept alive in the traditions of Robin of the Green Wood, Puck, Robin Goodfellow and Herne the Hunter.

This Green Man is in the very souls of Cheshire folk; he is in the hills and the dales and the forests. He still hunts in the remnants of the royal forests and he still takes their bounty; he rides the west winds and he strolls through the lanes with his bride Mary or Marian.

His face is to be seen in graven images and his soul can be sensed in the breeze. And in the merry month of May, with his Merry Men (or Marian's Men as some would have it) he gets up to all kinds of pranks or merry jests. Or so it is said and so it is understood to be. And it has been understood to be for many centuries for, after all, that is what a-Maying is all about, isn't it?

When Knutsford first started A-Maying, Noah would have been a lad. We now know of the traditional May Day ceremony at this Royal town, but it goes back far longer than anyone would care to hazard a guess at. True, there was a strong Victorian revival and that is what we now see, in the main, but it was purely and simply that – a revival. It was a tradition for many a a year and when the locals crown a young girl as Queen of the May (as they do now) they are worshipping the virgin. When the Maying ceremony became strong again in the late nineteenth century our Victorian ancestors realised they had not quite got it right and revitalised Jack, or Jack in the Green, the Green Man. Here is the symbol of vegetation who is born, gives forth his bounty then dies – only to be reborn in Spring the following year. Cheshire sired the legend of Gawain and the Green Knight, when the Arthurian hero decapitates the Green Man in Winter; a Celtic imagery associated with the Cult of the Head. Here is Jack taking part in the seasonal death and resurrection ritual; and it is Jack who leads the parade in Springtime at Knutsford, followed by the young girl and her attendants. Here he is Jack of the Wood as Robin is of the Greenwood; they are of the same ancestry are Jack and Robin.

The last time I visited Knutsford, in 1994, I had a chat with the man whose responsibility it now is to be Jack in the Green. He was named Bill Mullins, a resident of Knutsford, who works for Macclesfield Borough Council's Refuse Disposal Department. In fact, my cousin Stanley is his boss. This was Bill's seventh year as Jack and when I asked why he was doing it his reply was only too familiar. It was a reply I had been given at Antrobus when I asked one of the Soulers why he was carrying on with the ritual and it is a reply I was given when researching for another book (Staffordshire – its Magic and Mystery) at Abbotts Bromley by one of the Horn Dancers.

Knutsford's "Jack in the Green", Bill Mullins inside his suit of greenery before leading the Knutsford Royal May Day parade in 1994.

Bill Mullins said that, quite simply, someone had to do it and he wanted to keep the tradition alive. It was certainly hard work, for the frame and the greenery weighed very heavily and the parade around Knutsford inside the wicker-type basket of greenery certainly made him sweat.

Bill Mullins, left, before he became Jack in the Green, right.

In a book written in 1801 by J. Strutt entitled *Sports and Pastimes of the People of England* there is a description of the May festival. He mentions that chimney sweeps singled out May the first for their festival (and aren't sweeps supposed to be a sign of fertility at a wedding even now?) He said: "Some of the larger companies have a fiddler with them, and a Jack-in-the-Green, as well as a Lord and Lady of the May, who follow the minstrels in great stateliness, and dance as occasion requires. The Jack-in-the-Green is a piece of pageantry consisting of a hollow frame of wood or wicker-work, made in the form of a sugar-loaf, but open at the bottom, and sufficiently large to receive a man. The frame is covered with green leaves and bunches of flowers interwoven with each other, so that the man within may be completely concealed, who dances with his companions, and the populace are mighty pleased with the oddity of the moving pyramid."

The description of a wicker type basket of greenery made my mind draw comparison with the Wicker Man of the Celts. This was a construction of branches (just like Jack o' Knutsford) in which there was placed a persons or persons. Here the differences become apparent for the Celts then burnt their sacrificial victim as a symbol of rebirth. They don't burn their man in green at Knutsford any more but he is a symbol of death and rebirth just like the Celtic Wicker Man.

Cheshire's Green Knight

Strongly associated with the Green Man ethos is a 14th Century poem written in North Midlands and Cheshire dialect called Gawain and the Green Knight. It is set, so most now believe, in the Wirral and in Central Cheshire over to the hills of the East and finally at a magical and mystical spot only a stone's throw over the border in Staffordshire; a spot that used to be in Cheshire and was most certainly owned by the Earls of Chester.

A number of scholars far more worthy than I believe it was written by a Cistercian Monk and that it was undoubtedly the retelling of a pagan story associated with death and rebirth and the Celtic Cult of the Head.

Briefly, the story is of Gawain who meets the Green Knight

described as "Full fierce he was to sight and all over bright green" as Arthur and his knights settle down for a Christmas feast. The Green Knight, or Green Man as I think he should most certainly be visualised, challenges all comers to a blow-for-blow contest. Only our hero has the heart to face him and cuts off the Green Man's head with an axe but this doesn't kill him, he simply picks up his head and the head tells Gawain that he must travel to the Green Chapel in one year's time when the blow can be returned, as are the rules of the contest.

The Green Knight or Man, in this contest, was in all probability the fertility symbol who still heads the parade at Knutsford; he epitomised the earth itself making annual sacrifice and wanting in return the acknowledgement of living things and also trust and love. This Winter Game took place at the Yule time when the earth is dead and is awaiting rebirth. Each year the earth makes sacrifices and each year puts its trust in man to give the same. Man used to give the same in the form of sacrifices and these sacrifices were oft times made in baskets or containers of greenery and represented the Green Man. Here he represents Winter and he made the ultimate challenge to the representative of Summer, Gawain.

The epic continues and the seasons begin to turn. Sir Gawain roams across the Wirral peninsular and then comes into Cheshire and across to the manor of Swythamley – owned in those days by the Cheshire family of the De Traffords who were in charge of that part of the royal hunting forest. Here he comes across the Green Knight again but not before he is tempted by the Green Man's wife three times and finally accepts a sword belt from her – a green one. Eventually he is taken to the Green Chapel (which is a place called Lud Church, deriving its name from the Celtic God Lud) and the Green Knight appears. Gawain prepares for the fatal blow that he owes but the Green Knight merely nicks his neck, saying this is because he failed at the last and accepted the green "baldric" or belt.

Near to this spot was a Cistercian abbey called Dieulacres which had been founded by white monks from near to a ford across the River Dee at Poulton just upstream from Chester. They had been told to go to the eastern border of Cheshire by the Earl of Chester who himself had been told to go to this spot in a dream.

This was the furthest outpost of his Cheshire empire inside the Forest of Lyme, the dividing forest of the Palatine with the rest of the world. The monks had been having trouble with the marauding Welsh and this was as far away as possible that the holy men could be placed.

It is highly probable that the saga was penned by a monk, for in those times they were the clerics, the men of letters. Few others could read or write. And, because of the dialect and because of the locations it is a good bet that this monk, or monks, came from the Abbey of Dieulacres – that far outpost of Cheshire. That monk was re-telling the battle of summer over winter, of re-birth, of fertility. And that monk, who was living in a cloistered building amid the green woods, was re-telling the tale of the Green Man.

There is also the tradition that in 1379 the Abbot of Dieulacres was involved in some dark deed whereby a local gent was beheaded on the moors close by the abbey. The Cult of the Head re-born.

The Green Head

Just as the second world war was unfolding, Lady Raglan, who was a prominent anthropologist, wrote in *Folk Lore*, Volume 50, that in the year 1931 she had been shown a carving in the roof of a church. She said it was of a man's face, with oak leaves growing from the mouth and ears and completely encircling the head. It seemed to her that this was a "Green Man" who appeared in churches throughout the islands and throughout Europe. She recorded that these foliate heads had, in the main, oak foliage sprouting from their heads. This is a tree that was worshipped by the Celtic tribes and a tree associated with the Spirit of the Green Wood – Robin. There was also, she noticed, a predominance of ivy, also sacred. She sought to give these faces a name and attempted to find from what person they derived. She wrote: "The answer, I think, is that there is only one of sufficient importance, the figure variously known as the Green Man, Jack-in-the-Green, Robin Hood, the King of May, and the Garland, who is the central figure in the May Day celebrations throughout Northern and Central Europe." She added that in England and in Scotland the most popular name for this figure was Robin Hood.

She made mention of Sir James Fraser's oft-quoted work *The Golden Bough* in which he theorised concerning the sacrificed god who was chosen to reign for a year then beheaded and hung on a tree. Robin Hood's part as the annual victim in the cycle of vegetation has been taken further by others (E.O.James, Seasonal Feast and Festivals, Thames and Hudson, 1961).

So where can we find the decapitated head of the Green Man in Cheshire?

At the Parish Church in Audlem, as you enter the front porch, there is a head on the right hand side. Its face is blackened with so many hands touching it over the years – surely a sign of touching for luck, a ritual so often still enacted by us all? Don't we touch wood, for instance, for luck? Audlem derives its name from being within the Forest of Lyme – the Cheshire boundary forest. The Green Wood and the Green Man together.

The church at Audlem describes this head as a Jack in the Green.

Nantwich Parish Church has a Green Man to greet you as you enter its portals. Look above you as you walk in. Look up to the high ceiling and there it is. The official guide calls it a Jack in the Green, and there are others about the church.

Over the other side of Cheshire at Bramall Hall – once one of the homes of the Foresters of the Royal Hunting Grounds, the Davenports, there is a wonderful example of a Green Man on one of the external walls of this typical black and white Cheshire house. Surely this must have something to do with the owners being in charge of the green wood?

An illustration of the Green Man foliate head at Bramall Hall. It can be found in the woodwork on the exterior of the building.

And then slap bang in the heartland of Cheshire, at Barthomley, there is a Green Man or a Jack-in-the Green as the church likes to call it, on a wall outside the building. This is built on a high hill and this hill which was an ancient burial mound long before the Christians came to Cheshire. It was, and is, known as Barrow Hill. Here, the Green Man was worshipped before that Great Man who was sacrificed on the wooden cross. There are others in Cheshire, and perhaps some day someone will make a note of them all and also make comparisons.

Hilary and I did not come across the Barthomley Green Man by accident, but it has to be admitted that we were unaware of its existence up until the time that we were guided there one day. Let me explain. During June of 1994 we set out one sunny morning to visit Nantwich to call to see our friend Derek Hulland (with the intention of dropping off a photograph of the Image House at Bunbury among other things) and then going on to Sandbach. Derek's shop was not open when we arrived (he had gone to the bank, we subsequently learned, and had got into conversation with a number of people on the way) so we decided to set off for Sandbach to inspect the Saxon crosses and to enjoy the excellent market there. On our way into Crewe the road signs showed the main road was closed and there were diversions so, as we often do, we placed out trust in being guided to where we should go. We turned the car off the main road and soon found ourselves in delightful and glorious Cheshire heartland and, after turning here and turning there, arrived at Barthomley. This seemed the perfect excuse to sample the lunchtime fayre at that picturesque thatched and black and white timbered hostelry so often pictured on books about the delights of Cheshire villages. But it was closed. The one lunchtime it is not open is, so we discovered, Thursday – and that was the day we had arrived there.

I had wanted to show off the interior of that pub to Hilary because the last time I had been taken there was by two close friends who live in Crewe Green and I had been enthusing about the place ever since. I had had the delightful honour of meeting Oliver Horrocks, the Rector, who had been sitting by a roaring fire and partaking of a small glass of ale. We had a wonderful chat over lunch and I was rather hoping he, and lunch, could be enjoyed again. But it was not meant to be.

A fine example of a foliate head at Nantwich Parish Church. The building houses a number of extremely interesting carvings, some that defy description. I would recommend a visit.

Had our Nantwich friend been in we would not have gone on towards Sandbach and then been guided to Barthomley. Had the pub been open for lunch we would not have paid a visit to the church but, because of these events we found ourselves looking around the church dedicated to St Bertelin, or Bertoline, the Mercian Prince who became a Hermit after his wife and baby were devoured by wolves. We had paid a pilgrimage to the spot where he became a hermit and which became a healing site the year before during research for a book on Staffordshire (it is at Illam on the Staffordshire and Derbyshire borders) and this is still a place where healing can be carried out. There is a healing well and a healing tree at that spot and it has been described as a place where the Earth Spirit is at hand. This description rather fits Barthomley also, I feel.

Anyway, circumstances found us strolling around the Church on top of the hill at Barthomley and there we saw the Green Man, perched on top of a stone pillar on an exterior wall of the church. Growing around it was fresh ivy.

Jack in the Green on the exterior of the church at Barthomley.

There are others in Cheshire. One has all but been erased at the church of St Oswald at Malpas and there is a fine one in the Parish Church of All Saints at Daresbury. It is carved into a Jacobean screen. There is more Jacobean carving at Daresbury and the oak pulpit is a fine example and was something that caught my eye there for there are some more "fertility symbols" other than the Green Man depicted there, perhaps a sign that the Old Religion was suppressed but not defeated.

Whether Robin Hood, that now legendary Man in Green, was ever a real person is extremely doubtful. I know that Nottinghamshire people would perhaps dispute this as they have managed to create a thriving tourist industry out of him, but I feel that they have no stronger a case to claiming him as their own than any other county in England and that certainly includes Cheshire. He was the spirit of the green wood, the fertility symbol showing the triumph of life over death, good over bad. He was everyone's hero and he belonged to everyone.

Not that Cheshire hasn't staked a strong claim to him, for in a ballad entitled "The Merry Geste" dedicated to the Earl of Chester, he is very much a part of the Forest of Macclesfield and Will Scarlet, said to be his cousin in the rhyme, is from "Maxfelte Town" where he was "born and bred". This is Macclesfield, and Macclesfield was part of the royal hunting forest used by the Cheshire Earls and, ultimately, owned by the Crown.

Robin and Will were great bowmen, adept at the longbow, and it was the men of Cheshire who won the French wars for their King because of their skill with this weapon. These men were good and they certainly knew it; they were almost above the law because of their usefulness in battle. Their bows made of yew and, some say, grown in the Cheshire churchyards, were the ultimate weapon of the day. They could put two fingers up to almost anyone ... especially the French, for it was during these wars that the bowmen first used the two-finger salute as a sign of derision and of victory. Whenever a Cheshire bowman was captured his bow fingers, the two fingers on his right hand, were cut off by his enemy. Whenever the bowmen fired a volley at the French they followed this by the two-finger salute to show that their firing strength was intact.

And at Mellor Moor there are two ancient stones or crosses known as Robin Hood's Picking Rods, and sometimes Robin Hood's

Picking Pegs ... stones that have been used at one time to tap into the earth spirit. These stones, like the Bridestones just inside the Cheshire border by Bosley Cloud, have been used as sites for wedding ceremonies in days past. Few people at one time could afford to be married at a church and a ceremony of jumping over brushes or brooms of twigs would be held at a site associated with fertility. This is how the phrase "married over the brush" came about; the bride wearing a garland of flowers on her head (a band of green willow used to be worn to denote a woman's husband or boyfriend had gone away to war).

Robin, the Green Man or call him what you will, was married, or had as his sweetheart, the Maiden called Marian. Her name, as we have seen, derives from Mary which was the title given by the Church to the Holy Mother who had, in earlier times, been known as Bridget. It is from this name that the Bridestones (Bridget's Stones) derives. And it was at these stones that the brides would come to be married.

4

Dance of the Witches

Witchcraft means many things to many people. It can be a source of good, it can be something to be held in awe or disdain and it can be the Anti-Christ ... the work of the devil. The three weird sisters asking where they should meet again before Macbeth makes his appearance in the Bard's play were the Elizabethan idea of haggard old women concocting their evil potions. They were not flying high on hallucinatory drugs although they may have been brewing them.

In the late Middle Ages the witch scares began and continued until the 1700s. Pretending to possess powers of the occult was an offence against the Church; it was sorcery and it was something for the Church to deal with until the whole thing got completely out of hand and anyone's neighbour who happened to look like the perceived witch or just happened to have cross words with a vociferous person was likely to be accused of witchcraft. They weren't exactly burnt at the stake here in Britain but they were drowned – in ducking or cuckold stools – and they were starved, imprisoned, tortured and flogged. They were also hanged. One estimate gives 70, 000 being hanged during the reign of James 1.

It was only in the 1950s that the Witchcraft Act was finally abolished by Parliament and only then, for instance, could the Spiritualist Church's Mediums practise within the law. During the Second World War a well known Medium was incarcerated and stood trial under this ancient Act. In other words, it was a question of don't talk or try to talk with someone who is dead or you could go to jail.

There has always been a form of hysteria associated with witches or with the witch-finding that was commonplace at one time. Indeed, we still use the phrase "a witch hunt" to denote an unnecessary persecution. There were many zealots in the latter Middle Ages who made a tidy living out of seeking so-called witches. Matthew Hopkins the Witch-finder General charged very high prices for his services – seeking a witch, making him or her stand trial and overseeing the punishment. As he only got paid by results it comes as no surprise that he usually managed to get a result. This man could find the Mark of the Devil on anyone he chose. This was usually a birthmark or blemish or even a mole. Not a difficult task.

The people who were called witches in those days could (as I hope I have demonstrated in other books) have been herbalists or just the old lady who had the knowledge of how to deliver a baby. Most out-of-the way places had someone wise in the ways of healing. It was a necessity and these Wise People – a Wise Man or Wise Woman – were used by local people to considerable advantage. I was fortunate in having a Great Aunt who was a Wise Woman and she was fortunate in living after the hysterical witch hunts otherwise it would have been a fair chance that at some time she would have been accused of sorcery.

The theory was that if anything was against the normal run of the mill then it was because the black arts were being dabbled with. Then it was anti Christian and, therefore, of the Devil. It was sorcery and the powers used were, therefore, occult powers. These powers came, it was supposed, from the Anti-Christ. Persecution and paranoia went hand in hand.

Later, when the dust had died down, certain people realised they could use the powers associated with witchcraft to their advantage – they could blackmail the gullible by threatening to put a curse on their cattle or on their family or do some other dark deed if they were not paid. This became known as Casting the Evil Eye and these dark deeds became the work of the Black Witches – the baddies. To the rescue could come the goodies – the White Witches. These were the people who used their knowledge only for good – the Wise People who were about in most Cheshire villages up until the turn of the Twentieth Century.

In fact, there are still some about today. I have met them. I have told before of the Wise Man who I first crossed paths with after the Great Flood that devastated Wildboarclough in May of 1989. I met him after the Wild Bore (the torrential river) had subsided and he was collecting silt from the river bed to be used for healing skin ailments. I am, I'm pleased to say, a strong friend of his to this day.

There are still a number of people who are healers, whether they be spiritual healers using the laying on of hands or people who make others feel better just by their very presence. These are the best healers of all. And there are still people who are visited because they can cure with herbs and other potions.

People around Bunbury may very well know to whom I refer in this context.

There are in fact, a number of people who practise the Craft to this day and Cheshire is by no means short of them. These are, in the main, well-meaning folk with a strong wish to help their fellow human beings and long may they reign. Unfortunately, there are also a few people who attempt to use, or pretend to use, the dark forces. Thank goodness they are hardly ever successful and thank goodness they are in the minority.

Being both a newspaper journalist and also a writer and broadcaster on the supernatural and the mysterious it is, perhaps, not surprising that I have come across both types. And I have no hesitation whatsoever in saying that those I respect and admire are those who use their powers for good; the White Witches. The real ones, that is. Not the ones who pretend and play at it.

The Edge of Darkness

My first brush with witchcraft came around Hallowe'en of 1965 when I was a cub reporter in Wilmslow on one of the two local newspapers circulating in both Wilmslow and Alderley Edge at that period. A colleague of mine, Phil Smith, was assigned to cover a story about the weird goings-on at Alderley Edge and I made sure I was around. This was right up my street.

All Hallows Eve used to be feared as the time when winter begins and the dead roamed the skies. It was a time when those who practised real witchcraft held high revels as a method of keeping alive pagan beliefs and customs.

For a number of years there had been tales of people holding weird rites on The Edge – that wooded and mysterious spot on the escarpment overlooking the Cheshire Plain – at the Eve of All Hallows, or All Soul's Eve. It was here that local tradition had for so long hinted at strange happenings and it was here that journalists and members of the public were to encounter strange events on a windswept Hallowe'en Sunday around midnight.

Surprisingly, or not surprisingly, for three nights leading up to that Hallowe'en, local television stations had been showing so-called witchcraft activity on The Edge and so, equally not surprisingly, the local press trudged their weary way up to the wooded spot to see what was going on.

I have kept a cutting from the *Wilmslow County Express* of the report of what took place and, thanks to the good offices of Mike Quilley the now editor of the *Wilmslow Express Advertiser* (as it is today) I am able to quote from it.

The front page had a dramatic picture of a lovely blonde 18-year-old lady, the "Witch Queen of the North", holding both arms aloft, with a dagger in her right hand. It was she who had brought the ceremony to a close when she stood on the altar stone and looked out over Cheshire and Manchester to "claim her domain". What she saw from that vantage point she "ruled".

The ceremony was conducted at a spot known as The Devil's Hole and, while high winds and driving rain lashed through the storm-torn woods the witches, who said they were of the white variety, summoned the spirits of their ancestors. Within a carefully roped-off circle they brought the midnight matinee to a close with a frenzied dance around four daggers that had been plunged into the earth.

"It's not a lot of poppycock" stressed one who said he was the 22 year old High Priest of South Manchester (a draughtsman by profession). "It's our religion. We come here to come into direct contact with the God powers which enable us to help people."

This ceremony followed three nights of televised "witchcraft activity" on The Edge. As a result of the "advance publicity" scores of people braved the weather and roamed The Edge in search of the witches. They were discovered at the end of a mud-packed road leading from the Wizard Hotel. When questioned, the group said

Queen of All She Surveys ... the Witch Queen of the North looks out from The Edge at Halloween.

that to them Hallowe'en marked the end of the year for their Elder. "By tradition he should be burned. We burnt an effigy earlier this evening in Manchester" one of them said.

There were five in that group but only three took part in the actual ritual. One was a new man who had not yet obtained his robe and the other said he had left his robe behind in Manchester by mistake.

A new man converted to the coven was a 38-year-old computer engineer who lived in Manchester. He said: "Witchcraft gave me something an orthodox religion could not." The High Priest was a 22-year-old clerk, who sported a beard. A former analytical chemist was the so-called Chief Elder of the Northern Witches. He said he had been a white witch since he was seven and it was he, he said, who should have been burnt that night.

Dance of the Witches, Alderley Edge.

Standing in the roped-off circle the three uniformed witches were spotlighted by headlights from two cars which had been carefully positioned. The two plain-clothed members stood solemnly outside the circle watching the ceremony.

They said that the object of the ritual was to raise what they called the cone of power. It is through this power, one of them claimed, they gain the power to help the people in need. "The sinister black magic has no part in it." he said.

After performing their rites, such as kissing each other's feet and the girl striding round the circle protecting it by waving a dagger and uttering memorised phrases the three danced what could be called a "white witch waltz".

"I did not feel foolish dancing" one of the three told the local newspaper reporter afterwards. "People may have been standing round snickering and giggling but we just put that down to them not understanding our religion. Look, if you go into a church and see a priest in his robes you don't think he looks foolish, do you?"

The ritual completed, the three asked the small crowd of watchers if they wanted to join the circle. "If you have a problem we can help you" said one. Seven people joined in. The five witches danced in a circle round them after giving each a kiss before entering the circle.

Finally, to end the event, the girl stood on a vantage point on The Edge, the sprawling lights of Cheshire and Manchester filtering away in the distance, to "claim her domain". According to what those present told Philip Smith: What she saw she "ruled."

It must be said that this was not the first instance of the press witnessing "witchcraft" ceremonies on The Edge. During September of 1962 a Manchester Evening News reporter and a photographer saw and photographed what was claimed to be an "initiation" there.

Whether these people who had been the objects of the Press's attention were "witches" in the accepted sense of the word or whether they were performing a ritual for a form of "religion" they had concocted themselves I will leave you to decide.

Now, many years later during each and every Hallowe'en, The Edge is heaving with revellers making much noise – some wearing masks and some generally making a nuisance of themselves. They stagger and trip in the October-black woods and they all hope to see something "scary." I fear they will not.

Reflections of Images

There is a story that has been told and re-told of the Image House at Bunbury. I hope I now have a new, and a little different, tale to tell of this house that is connected with witchcraft. The tale I tell is one that stretches coincidence to the realms of synchronicity but first it may be necessary to tell the accepted version of Bunbury's Image House.

The tale is as follows: there is a house on the outskirts of the village of Bunbury by the side of the Whitchurch Road. It is on what was Common Land and it is now called The Image House. This house, so local tradition has it, was claimed through Squatters' Rights, it being erected within a day and a night and smoke coming from its chimney by dawn. (My own family, who moved from Piggford Moor in Cheshire to the high rocks of The Roaches near Three Shire Heads did the very same thing some two and a half to three centuries ago, by the way, claiming their own Squatters' Rights). But to continue: the occupant – called Seth Shone in a book to be written later – was wrongfully convicted of poaching and he was deported to Australia for eight years. Upon his return he fashioned stone images of his accusers, the bailiffs and the gamekeepers, the judge, jury and the Lord of the Manor. He cursed them and he placed them around his house. Within the heads, so the tale says, he placed the carved stone head of the devil himself so that they would be forever cursed. Today there are just three images left intact at the house. What has happened to the others I know not, but believe some were sold.

The Image House at Bunbury as it used to be. It became Clock Abbot in *The Shiny Night* by Beatrice Tunstall. On the walls were stone figures and above the porch were images of a jackdaw, a fox and another face. Hanging beneath the porch were other stone heads, some of which I believe to be of Celtic origin.
There was another house below the Peckforton Hills opposite the marshy remains of Peckforton Mere and the cultivated ground that was once Ridley Pool that had similar heads and carvings at one time. J.Ennion.

An enlargement of three of the stone heads. The one to the right is clearly Satan.

So there we have it, a good story that has been told and re-told. It certainly provides a fine example of the way mimicry for magical purposes is very much a part of the make-up of human beings. There are countless instances from Egypt, Rome, India, Greece, Ireland, Scotland and other places of Image Magic. The use of a doll made from wax, or carved from wood or stone, to represent the "victim" has been, and is, commonplace. During the trial of the Lancashire witches in 1612, for instance, one known as Old Mother Demdike said the quickest and surest way to murder someone by witchcraft was to make a picture of someone in clay "like unto the shape of the person whom they mean to kill and dry it thoroughly, and when they would have them to be ill in any one place more than another; then take a Thorn or a Pin, and prick it in that part of the Picture you would so have to be ill; and when you would have any part of the body to consume away, then take that part of the Picture and burn it. And when they would have the whole body to consume away, then take the remnant of the said Picture and burn it: and so thereupon by that means, the body shall die."

This belief has been echoed this century. I recall that when some barracks, left over the from the second world war, were being pulled down during the 1960s in nearby Shropshire a clay image of an officer, stuck with pins, was discovered.

I had not intended to dwell too much on this particular aspect of Cheshire witchcraft, because I felt the story had been told and re-told in many books about "curious" aspects of this county. However, in May of 1994 I was with Dave Clarke and Andy Roberts, two internationally-renowned authors and investigators of the supernatural. They had been kind enough to travel from Brighouse in Yorkshire to address a meeting of a group of like-minded people. I have been given the privilege of being made President of "The Green Dragon Society" and before they gave their address to the assembled Society Andy asked me if Bunbury was far as he would like to visit the Image House. As he had to be back at Brighouse that night and it was early evening already I persuaded him against a visit but promised him that I would take a photograph and post it to him.

One of the images that remains - presumably representing one of the sheriff's men.

The following day I mentioned this to a friend of mine by the name of Derek Hulland, who is himself a well-known author and proprietor of an excellent antiquarian bookshop in Welsh Row, Nantwich. He is also one of the best-known "characters" in Cheshire. Anyway, away I went to Bunbury to photograph the house and was very disappointed to find only three images left. Where was the Devil's Head, I wondered?

Another chat with Derek was necessary and he told me of the book *The Shiny Night* written in 1931 (William Heinemann, London) by Beatrice Tunstall, a Cheshire lady. This book was an historical novel with its story woven around the Image House and she had named the maker of the images Seth Shone. This book would be a delightful find for anyone interested in the Image House but was very scarce indeed.

It was from then on that coincidences became curiouser and curiouser.

My phone rang, it was Derek Hulland from Nantwich. "You'll never guess what" he said

"What?" I asked.

"A couple who live on Bunbury Common have just this minute left my shop" he said "and I've got some good news for you."

"What's that?" I enquired.

"Well, for some reason that I can't explain, I felt I had to ask this lady and gent if they knew anything about the Image House. I've never met them before, they've never been in my shop before, but it felt the right thing to do."

"And?"

"And they certainly do know about the Image House. They've got a photograph of it with all the heads around it – oh, and they have a copy of 'The Shiny Night' as well!"

This couple, it transpired, would be delighted to let me copy the photograph and would be pleased to show me the book – but they wouldn't part with it. They were Mr and Mrs John Ennion and Derek had taken their telephone number. I dialled their number immediately after finishing the conversation with Derek and was invited that Sunday morning to their cottage on Beeston Moss. Hilary and I spent several lovely hours with them, being entertained right royally to coffee and cake and biscuits. I was ably assisted by John in copying the picture of the Image House while the ladies bathed in the sun in the cottage gardens.

And that was that, I thought. I am used to this type of meaningful coincidence occurring and must admit that I rarely bat an eyelid when it does. But it did not end there.

I had told myself that I must get a copy of this rare book *The Shiny Night* and started to visit book fairs and any second-hand book shops I could. But to no avail. Then, one Saturday morning, I awoke and the first thing to cross my mind was that I must go to a book shop in Leek in North Staffordshire where another author and historian named Ray Poole (and another person I am happy to be able to call a friend) is to be found behind the desk. So off I went and began to peruse the shelves. "Would it be here?" I asked myself and then felt compelled to look behind me at a row of books I had not seen before. There it was. *The Shiny Night* by Beatrice

Tunstall. This shop, on the corner of Stockwell Street and Bath Street, is a veritable Alladin's Cave for the book-lover and I really don't know why I hadn't tried there earlier; but that's the way it goes.

I had sent Derek a copy of the Image House photograph and had discussed the heads shown thereon. I did not think – and still do not think – that those heads were carved by any poacher. They are the work of a skilled craftsman and, I think, they are the work of a number of different skilled craftsmen. In fact, I think that at least one if them is Celtic. Could they have been dug up, I wonder, in the surrounding fields? There are some old burial mounds nearby and they may have come from there. Whatever the case, they are most certainly very expertly done and for a poacher this gentleman was a mighty fine stonemason.

Ah, and something else:

The phone rang again. It was Derek again.

"That picture of the Image House you sent me" he said, "has got a blemish on it."

"Yes, I'm sorry" I replied. "It's my fault, something to do with the way I copied it."

"Well, take a look at it." he said. I did. It was the shape of a howling animal, a banshee or a devil dog. A coincidence, I know; but then they always are. . .

A Pinch of Salt

There have been very few black or evil witches in Cheshire because of the amount of salt beneath the ground.

This, I have been told, is fact. The devil or anything to do with evil can always be frightened away by a dash of salt, the Cheshire tradition states.

Not that there haven't been a fair number of people accused of being sorcerers or witches but these were, in the main, at the time when zealous Puritans ruled the roost. There was once, according to a number of people I have met around Beeston, a group of people who used to use the wooded slopes of Beeston's crag for the purpose of playing at conjuring up evil spirits but that was thirty or more years ago and they have never been named. In Macclesfield, for example, there was once a lady who lived in an area called the Watercoates and, as I have mentioned before, was the subject of a newspaper report. It said that she often visited the writer of the article's home and she took great pains to warn him against Black Witches and to instruct him in the art of a White Witch. He wrote that he has sat for many an hour in her cottage watching her bake oatcakes and listening to her stories about Black Witches. She always had a small tub, or what she called a "dashun" of salt by the fire from which she threw a handful into the fire when anyone passed and looked into her cottage whom she did not like or whom she suspected of witchcraft. This took place over one hundred years ago, and shows the openness there was about this subject then. It would appear that quite a number of people could be suspected of the Evil Eye, although they ever knew of this themselves is another matter.

At Witton nearby to Northwich there was once a person called Mary Eaton. As far as I can gather she lived about the late nineteenth century and is said to have died around the time of the Boer War. She was the mother of nine children and was used by local people for midwifery and she would be consulted for any aches or pains they would have. A White Witch, in fact. According to a letter sent to a Henry James Ashton of Fairfield, Openshawe, Manchester, this lady wrote rhymes, charms or incantations on pieces of brown paper and sold them as cures. Whatever ailment the patient had was treated with a different rhyme. The sick person had to recite this rhyme before a full moon and, it was claimed, would then be cured.

In rural Cheshire, quite a few farmers and agricultural workers made shapes and figures from pieces of wheat and corn. These are known today as Corn Dollies and perhaps the greatest authority on them in Cheshire is Raymond Rush of Siddington. I would recommend him to anyone who wishes to make a study of Corn Dollies or, indeed, anyone interested in rural customs. These figures are, in the main, associated with fertility of the crops and their use can be traced back to Egypt and across Europe, but they were also used in Image Magic as well. The Dolly would, years ago, be shaped from the last stalks to be harvested and would have a garland of flowers placed around it; the harvesters parading with it in high spirits and aided by the ale they would no doubt have partaken of after their labours. But it has been known for people to make Image Dolls from corn, not doubt given the idea by seeing the Dollies in rural Cheshire. These Image Dolls were used, as we have seen, to cast evil thoughts onto the person they represented.

Farming communities feared the Evil Eye being placed on livestock by people known as Black Witches. This rare photograph of Yew Tree Farm, Poynton, where the school now stands, shows the milking of a prized animal. Poynton is now very much a commuter village but there used to live there a woman who could cast spells or charms. It is said that all manner of ailments from warts to whooping cough could be cured by her. She would, therefore, have been a White Witch who worked for the good of the community.

There are very few records of punishment afforded to the witches of Cheshire and there was not the zealous witch-hunting in this county that took place further north in Lancashire, although some of the Witches of Pendle were tried by the Bishop of Chester. A number of towns had their own Ducking Stools, a device like a chair on the end of a balanced pole and the poor person being placed in that chair and ducked into the water. If they floated they were guilty of witchcraft if they sunk they were not guilty. In other words, they were onto a loser either way. There is still a road in Macclesfield, at the rear of the railway station, that is known as Cuckstoolpit Hill (Cuckstowpit in Maxonian) that derives its name from this barbaric custom. Stockport possessed a ducking stool and, according to the late Raymond Richards of Gawsworth Hall in his superb *Old Cheshire Churches* two men were prosecuted at Dunmow in 1880 for trying to duck a witch and, he wrote, a suspected warlock was done to death at Sible Hedingham in 1863.

There has been mention before of the two witches from Rainow near to Macclesfield called Ellen, the wife of John Beech and Anne, the wife of James Osbaston. They were tried at Chester for practising "certain artes" from which "wicked and devilish acts" certain Rainow people fell ill and died. There were hanged at the Michaelmas Assizes of 1656 and buried in the corner of St Mary's by the Castle Ditch in the churchyard on October the eighth. With them was Anne Thornton of Eaton near Chester who was also hanged after being accused of witchcraft. It has been said that this spot at St Mary's was tended for several centuries afterwards and flowers appeared on the site. I have not been able to substantiate this, however.

It is not difficult to conjecture what the Rainow women were tried for. Obviously there was an illness of some kind at Rainow and they were blamed for it – perhaps rightly, perhaps wrongly. But the witch-hunt did not end with the two hanged women. Some six years later, according to Jane Laughton who wrote *Seventeenth Century Rainow* a claim was made that Kettleshulme, just up the road from Rainow, had both a witch and a wizard and this accusation was made by several folk who could neither read nor write. The accusation was subsequently withdrawn.

It has been said that the last person hanged for alleged witchcraft within this county was a Wildboarclough widow named Mary

Baguley. The lady was brought to trial at Chester on April 26th, 1675, having been accused of the murder of Robert Hall at Wincle the previous year. The murder is said to have taken place through "magic". Some thirty years previously another widow, Margaret Percival of Pickmere is recorded as having been cleared of "bewitching, killing and murdering" two people at Great Budworth and she was also accused of placing the evil eye on a farm animal, a pig, belonging to Ezekiel Lawrenson and being cleared of this also. This charge of placing a curse on an animal was very common and the threat of placing a curse on an animal was equally as common. As I have previously said, there was a lot of blackmail going on and a lot of gullible people about.

Belief in witchcraft has been strong throughout Cheshire; it has not be confined to the rural areas for the industrial areas have had their fair share of belief in the unknown forces. This has not died and it will not hide away. There are many who still, while not admitting to believing that there are good and bad witches, will be wary of this or that. This has been handed down to us by our forebears. It is in our genes and will always be so. But, while most Cheshire people can still feed from the rich and salty Cheshire earth, then perhaps it is only the good forces that will be allowed to show through. I hope so.

Wizards were not exactly the male equivalent of a witch. That has become a Warlock. Wizards were the weavers of spells and the men who had knowledge that could be termed supernatural; above nature's knowledge. They were few and far between and today are practically non existent although, some say, they still exist. Merlin the Magician, the Seer of the Celtic Arthur who, as we have seen elsewhere and in other works, still haunts The Edge at Alderley, was one. And Tattenhall, eight miles south west of Chester, had one. His name was William Dean who was known as the Tattenhall Wizard and he lived some time in the 1800s but just when I have been unable to ascertain. It has been said that he was the caster of spells and local people lived in fear of him. His house, near Church Bank, has disappeared – not surprisingly. Perhaps his spells were nothing more than curses in which case our wizard was a black witch who cast the Evil Eye. Today, we cannot say for certain.

Get a good tale about a witch and it is told and retold, as is the case with Church Coppenhall's famous Bridget Bostock whose story appeared in the 1800s in the *Gentleman's Magazine*. People would flock to her from all over the place, and Nantwich and Middlewich folk used her healing powers rather than consult a doctor – perhaps because she would never taken any money for her healing. She gained results through the power of prayer and the use of her own spittle. A mighty combination indeed. There are some who would class her as a witch but there are others who would say she was just one of many ladies in Cheshire throughout the centuries who have been handed down the healing powers. Yes she was most certainly capable of healing but so were many, many, others. What was different about her was that some enterprising person decided to write off to the magazine and she became a national celebrity while others just got on with their job – not as witches but as healers.

Over at Kelsall, again in the 1800s, lived "The Old Witch of Kelsall" who was a woman given this name for no more of a reason than, so it was said, she kept a toad as a pet. She was not even credited with any healing, but this lady whose real name was Alice Cawley was branded an "Old Witch" as we today would, unkindly, call someone the same name merely for being a little unusual. I feel she should never be entered into the list of Cheshire witches.

But one who most certainly should be is Mary Worthington who lived in a small cottage just off Little Underbank, Stockport, in the year 1873. She was, so it was said, a witch for she could manipulate people as she liked, probably through fear. She had a very good living because she frightened her neighbours into giving her money otherwise they would receive the evil eye. A tale was told in the Cheshire Daily Echo that she received money on a weekly basis from as many as twenty different people but there had never been one instance of anything untoward taking place. Perhaps she was just a confidence trickster.

And there are echoes of the ducking stools of old at Barrelwell Hill, Boughton, at Chester where it is said witches – or those suspected of being – were tied up in barrels and rolled down the hill into the River Dee. There were gallows on top of the hill and just down the road, at Stocks Lane, there was of course the local stocks for wrongdoers. These poor "witches" who ended up in a barrel in the Dee were guilty if they floated and ended up at the top of the hill again but this time swinging from a rope If they sunk, they were not guilty. And dead.

The Curse of Death

Before we leave our look at witchcraft and curses I have a tale to tell. It is a strange tale and one that I would not have believed except for the fact that the person who told it to me is a highly respected gentleman who has been President, Chairman and figurehead of many organisations in Cheshire and has been a prominent trader within this county since just after the second world war. He now lives in retirement in a delightful council-owned maisonette and he is what can be described as a normal person. Quite a delightful chap, in fact.

And he is also the subject of the Fakir's Curse.

As I have said, I have known this gentleman for many years and early in 1994 he paid me a visit. He had read one of my books and wanted to tell me something. He was the subject of a Curse that meant anyone who threatened him would die. And since the war, when this was placed on him as protection by a Fakir no fewer than eight people, all from Cheshire, had threatened him in one way or another and they had all, later, died. A coincidence perhaps. But a very strong coincidence. He related the tale to me and itemised the people who had died after threatening him. I listened for over and hour as he went through the story and then thanked him, but I had not written any of it down. It was a complicated tale and one that needed to be told again. He readily agreed that I could visit him at his home and bring along a tape recorder. This I did and I have his tale on tape. Anyone who wishes to hear it is most welcome.

Obviously I am not going to identify him or the people who have perhaps died. It would cause distress to relatives and in relating the story I am being deliberately vague about some times, places and people in order not to identify anyone. But please understand that he genuinely believes what he told me. I will leave you to judge.

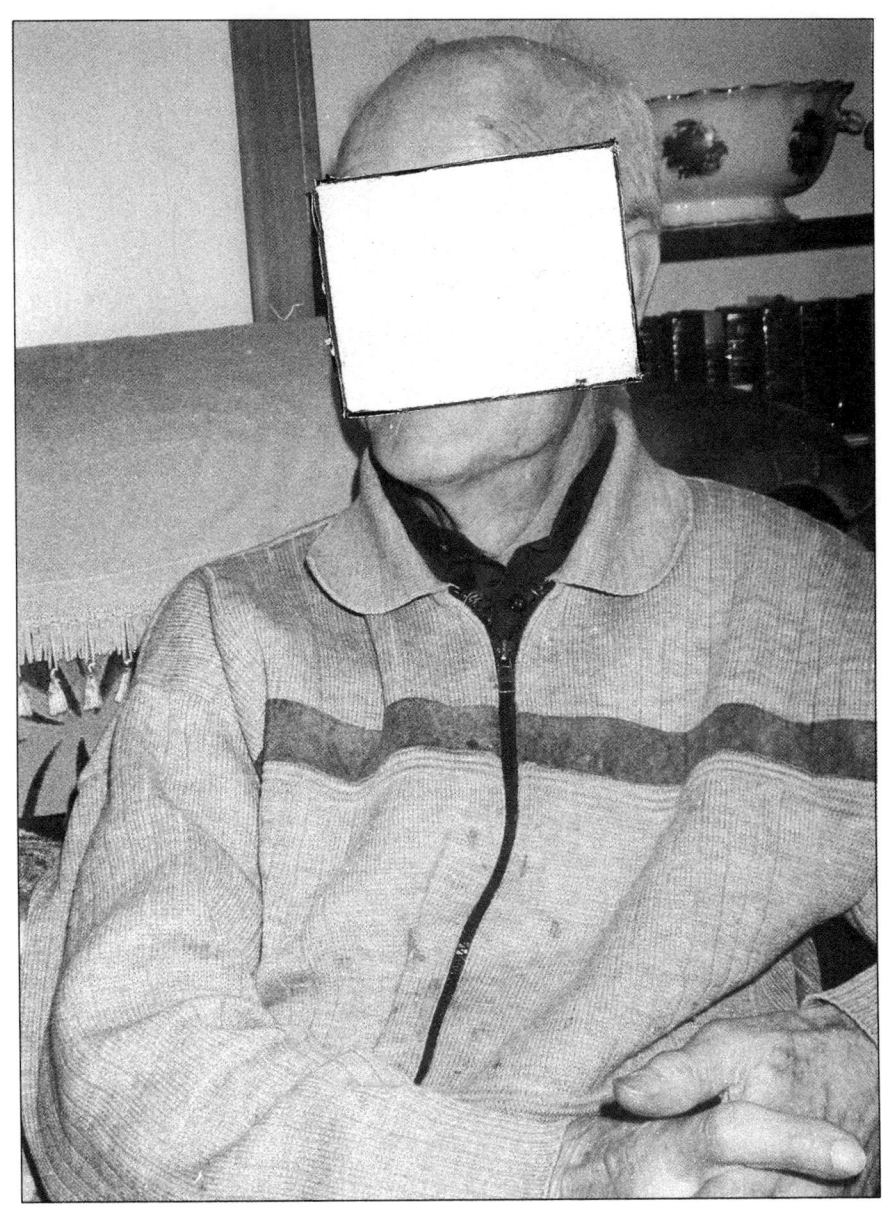

The man who was the recipient of the Fakir's protective curse. His face is deliberately obscured.

This is what he said:

During the second world war he arrived in India after being transferred to the RAOC and was promoted to Sergeant. He was stationed near to where the Rivers Jumna and Ganges join. Both are holy rivers. He decided to learn the language and paid for an interpreter to teach him the basics. One day he saw three or four sergeants talking to a Fakir who had a ring on the top of his head, his hair came down to his waist and was intertwined with a long piece of material. One of the sergeants said to our Cheshire man "It's fortune time!" and I asked: "Is he going to tell you you're a rich man?" and he replied "He doesn't seem too bad."

One of the sergeants was told by the Fakir that he could see nothing in his palm and the Indian pushed him away. "I thought perhaps he would not be here long because that chap would not turn money down but he would not take any off the sergeant."

He went on: "I put my hand up to him and he looked at it. I said I did not want to know about the future just tell me about the past, and he looked at my hand and said I came from England. That wasn't too hard and then he said I had three brothers and three sisters. I said that was wrong, I had only two sisters, and he got hold of my hand again and said one had died when a little baby. He said I lived near something very high and I did, a very tall factory chimney. I told him, again, that he was wrong about my sisters but he was adamant (and he later learnt from his mother that a sister had, in fact, died at birth). He asked me for my watch and held it in his hand and said that forever more it would be ten minutes fast (no matter what he did to the watch after that it was always ten minutes fast). I walked away from him and he said something else and I shivered, for I knew he had cursed me. I went to him and put my hands on his shoulders and said I was very sorry, he was a good man. He put his hands on my shoulders and said I would be alright. I gave him another rupee and he said that anybody who really threatened me moneywise, lifewise, or threatened anything of mine would die. As I walked away I felt something as though I had been belted on the back of the neck and I knew he had done something."

He added, "It is from that that various events have taken place and I can only say they were down to the supernatural."

He went on to explain how he from that time on happened to be in the right place at the right time to see events that only took place for a split second or two and were very unusual but the really unusual events began when he returned to England and, on leaving the army, came to a town in Cheshire.

He rented a property in the town and put a lot of money into it but was shocked when he received a letter from the council saying it was condemned and he had to get out. He wrote to his landlord who said he knew nothing about it but went to court against him. He died five days later.

He went to the solicitor who had drawn up the lease and asked him what was going on and told him he had given wrong advice and the solicitor said: "Show your face in here again and I will get the police and have you prosecuted". He died soon after making that threat.

He appealed to the County Court and the Judge gave him twelve months "stay of execution" to allow him plenty of time to find other accommodation and a Council official said to him afterwards: "Put a foot wrong and you're out. If you are not out quick enough the bricks will be around your head."

The man said to me that it was then that he thought about the Fakir's curse and wondered whether he could insure this man against death! He asked his insurance man who called weekly to collect the premiums and was told that it was not possible but the two chatted and he explained why he asked. Six to eight weeks later the insurance man came and told him the council official had died. "I shivered" he said "and immediately I could see the face of the Fakir".

He continued with his tale and said, "I used to take my dog onto a plot of grass every night and a man came up to me and said he had put his foot in some dog dirt. I told him I always watch my own dog and ensure it does not do anything where anyone could tread in it but he said he would put some arsenic in a steak and give it to my dog. Two weeks later he died."

He went on: "I was playing snooker and the ball was against the cushion so I put my foot on the floor and leaned onto the table. This man shouted and told me to stop and threatened me. I never gave it another thought but a couple of months later he was driving his car in a storm and a tree fell on top of it and he died."

And then there was the salesman at a garage. The man purchased a Commer 30cwt van for his business. A price was agreed but when he got the bill it was more than the agreed amount because of purchase tax being more than was said. "I went to see him and he told me to get out or he would throw me down the stairs" Later, he had a heart attack and died.

Later, he had an incident with a motor cyclist who kept driving alongside him and no matter whether he went fast or slow the motor cyclist stayed in the same position. He eventually managed to lose him at some traffic lights in the town and later he saw the bike rider with a group of others. The biker made a threatening gesture towards him and shouted. That evening he crashed and was killed.

It does not end there. There was the boss of the same Club where he had been playing snooker and one night the man was playing a one-armed bandit and was resting on a chair as he did so. The boss tapped him on his shoulder and told him not to do it otherwise he would be kicked out of the club. He later received a letter to say if there was anything like that again he would be suspended. Three months later the Club boss died.

Finally, he told me the story of how he befriended a lady with whom he used to dance with at another club in the same town. She was knocked about by her husband and one night when she came dancing there were bruises on her face. "She was in a right state" he said "and I told her that if ever she was in real trouble there was room for her at my house."

One evening she telephoned to say her husband had hit her again so he drove round and picked her up and took her back to his home where she stayed. Eighteen months later her husband threw bricks at the window and police were called. Some months later when the man was working in the garden he felt someone kick him. He turned and it was the husband who carried on hitting him. Eventually police arrived and he was arrested.

The husband became ill and some months later, he died, and when the man heard of the death he once again saw the Fakir's face in his mind.

The man concluded his story by telling me this: "All these are absolute coincidences but how many have you got to have before you start thinking there is something?"

He related some of the things he had seen after he had talked to the Fakir that were all coincidences as well, such as coming across a massive elephant leading a young elephant and the youngster holding its tail with its trunk and a massive snake with a frog in its mouth. The frog was screaming just before it was devoured. And he told of how he saw thousands upon thousands of flying ants hatch and a chimpanzee walking across the tree-tops of a huge tropical forest and a dozen poisonous snakes swimming together across a river – all events that are rare, and that few people will see in their lifetimes. To see them all within a short space of time was, he said, too much of a coincidence for him.

This "curse" has the same substance as the "evil eye" that was feared by many in Cheshire a while ago. A supposed practitioner of the black arts would place a curse on someone and, more often than not, the power of suggestion meant that person would most certainly suffer. The difference here is that the "victims" of the "curse" were unaware of the Fakir. I will leave you to decide.

5

Be weer of The Buggins

It was Saturday, the 18th of June, 1994 and Hilary and I parked the car in the main street at Tattenhall. The afternoon was sunny and there was a slight breeze blowing through the rambling roses that grew around the cottage doors of the quaint houses so typical of rural Cheshire.

A brass band could be heard in the distance for it was the occasion of St Alban's Church Fete. A typical Saturday afternoon in summer. A rural idyll.

We got out of the car and strolled up Church Bank towards the fete. Children were scampering about, elderly folk were sitting on the lawn taking tea and cakes and the band played on as the sun beat down. Wonderful. But we had not come to witness this, as magical as it was. We had come to visit the church because of another form of magic: earth magic, for St Alban's is on a strong earth energy line and the site upon which this church now stands, with the flag of St George flying proudly in the breeze on top of the tower, was a "pagan" site in pre-Christian times. But the tale of the earth line, or dragon line, is one for another chapter. It is what occurred when we were in the churchyard that we must look into.

We were strolling around the building that was, unfortunately, locked, when I was stopped in mid-conversation because I noticed a woman standing at the main entrance to the church and she was, I felt, staring at us. I turned to wish her a "Good Day" and she was no longer there. Nothing unusual for me or for Hilary (as readers of other books of ours will know, I'm sure) but Hilary asked me what she looked like. I described her as having been wearing a black dress down to her ankles and a white "bib" at her front.

"Was she wearing a hat?" Hilary asked.

"Well, no, she wasn't; at least I don't think so" I replied.

"That's odd" said Hilary, "for most women wore hats around and in Churches. Most still do."

I thought for a moment and tried to visualise her again but I could not recall her head at all, try as I might. A little more concentration and it became clear: I had been unable to recall anything about her head because she had not got one. She was a ghost, apparition, spirit ... call it what you will. Some would call it the Headless Woman, no doubt. Oh, and just for the record, there was a teenage girl in that graveyard with us at that time only she, also, was not from our world or plain. She, also was a "ghost" – although she did possess a head.

So there we have it, except for the fact that some time later Hilary was reading *The Cheshire Village Book*, a superb publication compiled by the Cheshire Federation of Women's Institutes (Countryside Books Berkshire, 1990) and in the section devoted to Tattenhall was the brief mention of the ghost of a headless woman who, according to the book, sat after dark by the Pool Head Field Gate on the Chester Road. This was not the spot I had seen my "headless woman" and there is no further description of her (although what better description could there be than she "had no head"?)

The publication gave a little rhyme, an old couplet, that said:
"Coom thou yarly, coom thou leet
Be wee of the Buggin at the Poo Yed Geet."

This good and solid Cheshire dialect says that whether you are there early or late beware of the Buggin at the Pool Head Gate. A Buggin is a ghost or spirit, and is the Cheshire form of Boggart or Goblin – the Hobgoblins – that are so mischievous. It is a variant of Bocan, a Celtic name for a ghost. They are akin to Puck and the Earth Spirit and they are akin to Earth Magic. There is more of this extremely interesting Earth Energy Line that travels through Tattenhall in another chapter but briefly, for fear of repetition, I must say here that on this line, just before it reaches Tattenhall, it travels over Hobb Hill – the hill of the earth spirits.

The church of St Alban at Tattenhall on the line of the dragon and where a "ghost" was seen.

I have told of these Earth Spirits to members of the Cheshire Federation of Women's Institutes on many occasions and church and school and village halls around and across the county have witnessed the spectacle of me showing these good ladies how to dowse for earth energy lines. And many of the members have related to me tales of their own particular ghosts. Before we leave the good ladies of the Cheshire Federation of Women's Institutes, I would here like to pay tribute to them for doing more than many to keep alive the traditions of Cheshire. I have had the pleasure of visiting many Women's Institutes around and across the county to give talks and have always been made to feel very welcome and have always been entertained right royally to a splendid cuppa and sandwiches and cakes. My thanks to you all, ladies.

A Hunting We Will Go

So just what, exactly, are ghosts?

I have the pleasure of knowing a person who lives over the border in Staffordshire who is a ghost hunter. He finds them by various means, including dowsing. His name is John Gilman and he has various theories about what is what is not a ghost. He is a fascinating man and someone whose work and theories I can heartily recommend. But what about my own views, I hear you asking.

Since we came down from the trees and began to be hunter-gatherers and began to destroy each other because of territory, possession or belief, we have been aware of that which has gone before. Visualisation conjured from the memory banks has always been easy and the dead have been venerated, especially those who had been leaders either because of their fighting capabilities or their mystic qualities – the Leaders of Men. Ancestor worship placed these on the pedestal of gods. Our Celtic ancestors kept heads of their great and loved ones; they pickled or preserved them in stone or clay vessels and would bring them out to talk to them or to consult in times of need. We still talk and consult through prayer and we still preserve heads, in stone or clay, on buildings. There are many on the gable ends of Cheshire houses and there are even more on the churches of Cheshire.

As people and their societies became more and more complex then the Places of the Departed became more extinct from the Here and Now. Those Elysian Fields were where the souls of the departed craved for and sometimes it was difficult to get there. The River Styx had to be crossed, for instance, and the ferry-man had to be paid.

At the Church dedicated to St Alban the Martyr at Tattenhall there was once a skeleton dug up close to the north wall. This skeleton was of a tall man and a coin had been placed underneath his head. Was this to pay the Ferry-man across the River Styx? It has long been a Cheshire custom to place a penny over the eyes of a corpse for this very purpose.

It became increasingly important to bury the dead in the proper manner, otherwise their spirits could not find their way to their heavenly resting places. Suicides and those hanged for crimes such as murder were often buried at crossroads so their souls could not find their way. Those accused of witchcraft were buried in unsanctified spots and their bodies buried back to front. There is a spot high above the Macclesfield Forest that I have discussed in previous works. It is known as Standing Stone and is on a crossroads. Close by is a field in which suicides were buried, back to front. Not only were they laid to rest the wrong way round but the spirits would have been confused by being at crossroads, it was thought.

Here I must ask you to forgive me for quoting from a book I have written concerning the Earth Magic of Staffordshire (Staffordshire: Its Magic and Mystery): these primitive attitudes towards the spirits or souls of the departed were kept alive over the centuries and our folklore and popular culture has ensured that these ghosts of the past remain to haunt us.

And, of course, there have always been those who can genuinely "see" the dead. Just pay a visit to a modern-day Spiritualist Church or have a word with a Medium. Better than that, just have a word with my wife!

Many dead people who have "re-appeared" have been those who have met their death in a violent or extremely unpleasant manner. They have left behind a strong energy that remains for others to pick up. These patches of energy, often preserved in the stones of buildings or in the earth itself, retain the memory of that which has happened.

Perhaps that is why headless men and women are seen. I can think of few more unpleasant ways of meeting death. There is a pub known as The Headless Woman near to Hockenhull Hall and for many years there was the carved figure in its gardens of a woman holding her head. I believe its fate was to be stolen and I also understand that it was, in fact, the figurehead of a ship. However, unusually for a seafaring figurehead, this woman wore a white apron, as can be seen from the rare photograph reproduced in this book. The story of the Headless Woman is that a part of

Cromwell's soldiers, engaged in hunting down the Royalists in the Chester district, visited Hockenhull Hall but found that the family, being warned of their coming, had buried all their silver and other valuables and then fled for their safety leaving only a faithful old housekeeper in charge of the Hall, thinking it unlikely the soldiers would do her any harm. The soldiers, being incensed at finding nothing of value, locked up the housekeeper in a top room and proceeded to torture her to make her tell them where the valuables were hidden. She remained faithful and was finally murdered by the soldiers cutting off her head.

The Headless Woman as she used to be in the pub of that name. J.Ennion.

Tradition says that afterwards, on numerous occasions, she was seen carrying her head under her arm, walking along the old bridle path between Hockenhull Hall and the spot where it comes out on the Tarporley Road near to the pub now known as The Headless Woman.

And there is another spot that was witness to an extremely unpleasant incident where the memories of the dead still haunt. It is at Barthomley, that picture-postcard village that epitomises all that is good about Cheshire ... or does now.

This also took place during the Civil War when Cheshire really was The Divided County as Derek John Brownsword Hulland (what a wonderful name for a fine Nantwich character) described it in his book published by himself in 1994. At this quaint spot stands the church dedicated to the Mercian Prince St Bertoline, or St Bertram, who became a hermit after his wife and daughter were devoured by wolves (can it be a coincidence that the brook running through the village is called "Wulvarn" and was near to the spot where the last wolf in England was supposedly killed? Revenge indeed.) This church has the unpleasant nickname of the Church of the Massacre and received this title because, during the Civil War, a number of villagers fled to the tower for refuge. They had, it is believed, shot at the Royalist Army who were coming from Nantwich and the story is told that they were led by the son of the Rector. All the villagers who were in the tower were smoked out by Cromwell's men and twelve of them were killed, the remainder were stripped and all manner of diabolical deeds were committed. Is it any wonder, then, that people still hear the screams on some evenings and is it any wonder that people have not only smelled smoke when there have been no fires around – usually in the height of summer – but have also seen the smoke haze as well? I know two people who say they have seen souls in torment at the spot and when Hilary and I visited there one afternoon in June of 1994 she was aware of the distinct aroma of something burning. At first we thought it was a pipe being smoked – although I could not smell anything similar – but there was no-one to be seen and Hilary was not, at that time, aware of the story of the massacre. She is now.

A Prestbury Tale

In November of 1993 I received a letter from Mrs Myra Oldfield of Moran Crescent, Macclesfield. In with the letter was a cutting from a Canadian newspaper, The Star, published on Ontario, and dated

September the eleventh, 1993. Mrs Oldfield asked if I would be interested in the cutting, and I most certainly was. The cutting had the headline: "English village haunted" which would hardly warrant a second glance over here, but then the content proved of great interest. It said: "From the Black Abbott to the Galloping Cavalier to cheerful Old Moses, the village of Prestbury in England has been named the most haunted place in the world by the British Psychic Research Society". Do they mean us, I wondered? This, in fact, referred to Prestbury in Gloucestershire (See "Walking in Haunted Gloucestershire", Florence E. Jackson and Gorden Ottewell, Sigma Leisure). Mind you, I would not have been surprised if it had referred to the Cheshire Prestbury!

Now, I am the Editor of the local newspaper that reports on happenings of all kinds within the village of Prestbury. It has been reporting on anything that has occurred in that village since the year 1811 and I have been a local journalist thereabouts for 30 years (at the time of writing this). I know that not everyone is going to rush for the phone and get in touch with the news desk of their local paper to report they have seen an apparition or whatever. After all, most of us have been educated NOT to believe in ghosts or suchlike. They are the product of a distorted mind, it used to be said. People in their right minds do not see such things, do they? Of course they do: Prime Ministers, members of our Royal Family, University Professors, Nuclear Physicists, film stars and many others in the public eye have all "come out of the closet" and made public the fact that they have seen something they cannot explain. But many more thousands of ordinary people like you or me have also seen something. Whatever it may be.

In her letter, Mrs Oldfield had an interesting story or two about Prestbury which I am happy to relate. She was especially interested in the cutting she had received from Canada because her grandmother had lived there in a cottage in the churchyard itself, behind the church. She went to Butley Hall when she was thirteen years old as a "tweeny" which is what maids were called when they went into service. She worked her way up to parlour maid and when she was 20 years old she fell in love with the new gamekeeper, who was a Scot named Angus Campbell and they married. Lord and Lady Brocklehurst from Butley Hall provided them with a large cottage in the woods down Bluebell Lane, Tytherington. Mrs Oldfield's grandmother used to cook breakfasts for the huntsmen who used to come to Butley Hall for the shoots and her grandfather, the gamekeeper, arranged these events and looked after the pheasants for the shoots. Whilst living in the cottage they had four children, three girls and a boy, and it was a lovely furnished house and the children had a lovely life there. Then her grandfather was taken ill when he was aged 40 and the cottage had to be vacated to make way for the new gamekeeper. They had to find somewhere to live and Prestbury Parish was so concerned for them that they found them the cottage in the churchyard. It had been empty for years but was made habitable and the villagers got together and found bits of furniture for them to go in this four-roomed house in the graveyard.

Prestbury in the 1930s

Her grandmother took work cleaning the church and even washing the surplices. Mrs Oldfield wrote that she often wondered where her gran actually hung the washing out to dry (was it in the graveyard?) She also wrote to me that she wished she had listened more intently to what she was told of all this at the time, but then she was only small. How many of us can say the same, I wonder? I certainly wish I had listened more to what I was told about my family. It was only in the later years of many of my relations that I took it upon myself to retain the memory of those who had gone before and I am thankful that I was guided to do so before it was too late.

But to continue with Mrs Oldfield's recollections: her grandmother took in a couple of roadmenders as lodgers but she only had a single bed for them in the back room and she slept in a double bed with her four children.

She used to make jugs of tea at weekends for the visitors to the church and she would set them out on cloth on the tombstones – the flat ones. "I don't know how they allowed her to do that" she wrote and added: "Her front door came out in the Bridge Hotel's lane that was there then. When the youngest girl was eight she died. Her name was Jessie – her mother's name was Maggie – and when Jessie died they found the water from the graves had been seeping into their water supply (the same water they had been making tea from to give to the visitors to the church). The Council had to condemn the cottage and so my grandma had to put all her belongings on a hand cart and it was pushed to Macclesfield with the three small children behind and she was found a one up and one down in Longacre Street and she got a job at Cameron's Shirt Mill in that street where she worked during the day and took washing in at night. It must have been awful for her but she did it."

It is the ghosts of people like her who should be remembered with affection and the ghosts of people like Lord and Lady Brocklehurst who threw out their gamekeeper and his family when he was taken ill who should be pitied; some would say their souls are now paying for this, who knows?

I had not heard these tales of Prestbury before, but I had heard it referred to as the Village of The Dead. The church of St Peter was the Mother Church of the area and, at one time, was the only place where people from miles around could be buried. A number of my own ancestors are there, including one who now rests near to the Saxon cross that contains a carving of the Prestbury Dragon – a depiction of the earth energy and its pagan attributes – defeated by the Christian church, usually in the form of one of two Dragon Slayers: St George or St Michael. Close by is Spittle House that used to be a "hospital" run by the holy men who lived in the village. The name Prestbury, it is commonly believed, derives from Priest's Town and there most certainly has been a collection of these Holy Men, probably monks, associated with the Mother Church for many centuries. Their place of healing at Spittle House on the banks of the River Bollin was used for leaching and blood letting, plus other ways of healing.

However, there is another theory about the origins of the place. Work with dowsing rods, pendulums and the open mind has revealed to a number of people that there was once a circle of stones at the spot where the church now stands. This is in itself not uncommon, most churches were placed on sites that had previously been where pagans or pre-Christians had worshipped. There are at Prestbury some strong earth energy lines, ley lines, dragon lines or call them what you will, that converge on the church site; and this, again, is not out of the ordinary. Many churches that had been founded on these previous sites of worship have earth energy lines going to them. These lines were, most probably, there before the Church itself. But at Prestbury the energy is not emitted from the area of the church itself. It has disappeared or, rather, has been suppressed. At many sacred sites – whether Christian sites or those like Stonehenge or Avebury – there is a strong energy field. Perhaps this is why they were erected at these spots. But at Prestbury there is nothing now emitted.

It has been conjectured that St Peter's was built on one of these lines for, unlike many churches, it is not built east to west. It is 22 and a half degrees out of true orientation and was done so, some think, to be on an earth energy line. It is also conjectured that once built upon that line there has been a considerable amount of energy placed there by pious and well meaning people to defeat the dragon and place the "dragon" back to where it belongs – under the earth. In other words, there is now a sleeping dragon under the church that will, no doubt, be defeated again, should it rise up, by Prestbury's own Dragon Slayer.

The name Prestbury may also denote a fortified community. Why should the monks have needed to be fortified, or defended? Who would have wanted, or dared, to have attacked them? Perhaps it was the Dragon, in the form of pagan or un-Christian people, who would or could have carried out these attacks to regain their sacred site of worship? After all, there was a fortified place of some description at the top of Castle Hill at one time. It was on the site of what used to be a farm at the top of Castle Hill leading to Mottram St Andrew. It is now White Gables but was known previously as Cocks Head. Until the turn of the twentieth century Cocks Head Wood was nearby but was cleared in 1915 for the war effort. Cock or Cop meant top. Castle Hill was previously Castle Lane.

Perhaps Prestbury people and members of the Psychic Research Society should be experiencing the ghosts of the Celtic Druids, for it is quite likely that the spot was once a Sacred Grove where these Holy Men worshipped. Perhaps St Peter's Church was on the very site of the Sacred Grove that would have been within a forest, and usually a forest of oak trees. Oak Tree House is in the angle of Castle Hill and Chelford Road and there was a well there at one time and it was said that water from it was the sweetest there could be. People would go to it and fill their pots and pans and, in later years, its water was said to make the best cup of tea imaginable. Here we have a few more clues to the possibility of a Sacred Grove in the oak forest for one of these special spots was usually associated with a special stream, well or spring and undoubtedly the water that came from the well at the house that had a special oak tree there at one time (it had to be special to be named after it).

The Haunted Town

Just down the road there is a town that could be a joint contender for the most haunted township stakes. Its name is Macclesfield and it is on a par with another Cheshire town, Nantwich, for the top haunted town title.

As the Editor of the local newspaper in this fair town it is hardly surprising that I should have made a note of many of the sightings of ghosts, spirits or whatever we wish to name them. There have been instances of hauntings at pubs, houses, garages and at the Macclesfield Borough Council offices among others. And I recall that during the early 1980s there was a Council-owned bungalow that was possessed with a poltergeist and a Church of England Vicar performed the exorcism ceremony to rid the building of that wayward spirit.

Some years later, in February of 1988, after performing an exorcism at a Weston Estate home, a ghostbusting cleric warned of what he termed "the dangers of the occult". At the same time he offered to bless the terraced home of Dorothy and David Moore in Lord Street where they and their four children had been haunted for three years.

Pastor Henry Drabble of Macclesfield's Calvary Church had that week been called upon to exorcise the home of a woman living on the Weston Estate where the occupant had been disturbed by a series of "strange experiences". He said afterwards, "There's a natural world where I can see you and you can see me. And there's a spiritual world in which some people report they have seen ghosts. I don't ridicule it. It's a disturbing fact."

He had offered to exorcise the home at Lord Street where David Moore, a 37 year old aerial contractor felt uneasy – as though being watched every time he went into the cellar. Dorothy, then 36 and an ICI clerk had seen the spectre of a little girl playing on the landing and someone or something shaking their bed at night. Their son, David, had been held down on his bed by a presence. Their other son, Andrew, was convinced he saw a man in a top hat and tails standing in his bedroom. The then teenager said, "I didn't have any curtains up at the time so there were no shadows".

I was once told by Mrs Hodgson, a Macclesfield lady, that number 10 Chestergate was haunted by the ghost of "Miser Hall". This man lived there in the early 1800s and was, as his name shows, someone who was very careful with his money. He was said to haunt the premises and when Mrs Hodgson lived there a maid was said to have remarked that she had seen him in the cellar "quite mad".

Inside the haunted house in Lord Street, Macclesfield.

And at the Chestergate premises of the Macclesfield Express, at number 37, there can often be heard footsteps at night. Many has been the time that a reporter or photographer or the cleaner has heard someone walk up the stairs but there has never been anyone or anything seen. There are people who will not stay in the building on their own.

Returning to Mrs Hodgson, she also told me that there was a house in Sutton, near to Macclesfield, which had a quaint ghost story associated with it. It was called "Hockley" and was inhabited by the Hine family who were Quakers. "My aunt" she said "who was then Miss Ellen Dunkerley became engaged to Mr George Hine, and she went to stay at the house. There were many stories told about the house and on one occasion my aunt said she was coming down to the evening meal and saw an old man sitting on the chest on the staircase. Footsteps were often heard in one of the rooms and when the house was sold to a Mrs Ardern, she was, I believe, unable to live in it because of the frequent appearances of the old man and the strange noises that persisted in the room."

In July of 1990 the staff of two adjoining premises in Mill Street, Macclesfield were scared by a series of unexplained events. To end their fear, the Institute of Psychic Research was asked to investigate. Lewis's Travel and Supasnaps staff were refusing to venture alone around the premises that used to be a pub. Travel shop manageress Caroline Arnold-Brown said that for more than a month loud bangs and bumps had disturbed them. "There were heavy footsteps walking from one side of the building to the other when nobody was upstairs. It happens quite often and we all hear it" she said and added "then things started to go missing. We put our umbrellas in the room at the back of the building to dry out one morning and they just disappeared and it was the same with a radio we had.

But things began to get worse when staff tried to find a way into an old cellar. They removed boards from the wall in what had become the kitchen and unearthed a tiny cubby hole but no entrance. They nailed boards back and shoved a large cupboard against it yet the next morning they found the cupboard had moved more than a foot away from the wall and turned on a slant and the boards had been loosened as if someone had tried to get out. Fearing they were going out of their minds staff went next door to

Supasnaps where employees there were relieved that someone else had heard the weird noises. A Supasnaps assistant, Emma Jelfs, said they heard a chair scraping on the floor upstairs when there was nobody up there and they often heard footsteps going right across the building.

That same year, staff at the Davenport Street premises of Kwik Fit were reported to be turning pale when their work takes them down to the cellar because they were convinced it was haunted. Some had run out in alarm after experiencing the "presence" and a frightened few had vowed never to set foot in the cellar again. Manager Alan Sladen admitted he was sceptical but said he felt the presence of the ghost when he went into the cellar to change a fuse. "I was feeling my way along the wall to find the fuse box and it was as if somebody was right behind me" he said and added, "I got out of there pretty fast and I never said anything about it until the day the auditor came tearing out of the cellar at a hell of a speed. Then an electrician fitting an alarm system had the same sort of scare. The cellar is normally the warmest place in the building but all of a sudden it gets really cold. Whatever the presence is, everybody who had experienced it has pointed to the same part of the cellar as the spot where they felt it.

And the company's regional auditor, Gordon Wright, said, "The first time I felt a presence, not very strongly, and on a couple of other occasions there was a feeling there was somebody down there. But one day I had a very strong feeling that I was not alone. I thought one of the lads had come down to see me but when I turned round there was nobody there. I just caught a glimpse of a sort of bluish haze before it disappeared."

At one time the building was the Old Royal Oak Hotel (to which I referred in a book *Myths and Legends of East Cheshire and the Moorlands*) and was at one time a popular meeting place for servicemen. During the second world war it was frequented by American servicemen.

Did something terrible happen in that cellar many years ago? The Institute of Psychic Research at the University of Nottingham decided to set up monitoring equipment there but, I believe, found little or nothing.

As it happens, I had written before that just by the Royal Oak there was a murder in one of the cottages, just along Davenport Street. A young woman was killed by a local man, Ernest Thorley, who was found guilty of the crime and hanged at Knutsford Jail.

This area was also the place where witches, or rather those thought of as being witches, were "ducked" in an evil contraption known as a ducking stool. The area is still called Cuckstoolpit Hill after this device whereby the accused person was placed in a seat and lowered into the water. If he or she floated then they were guilty as accused. If they sank, and presumably drowned, they were innocent.

And then there was the case of the ghostly Lady of Stuart House in Macclesfield. Stuart House is a concrete monstrosity of a building (to my way of thinking, anyway) that stands in King Edward Street, Macclesfield. It was leased by Macclesfield Borough Council on local government reorganisation in 1974 when authorities such as Macclesfield, Wilmslow and Knutsford found themselves as one Council. This, of course, happened throughout Cheshire and as I am writing this chapter I hear that there may be some more reorganisation of local government on its way. This is one ghost they should lay for rest once and for all. Anyway, the council ghoul made her appearance almost as soon as Stuart House became occupied in 1974. Her happy haunting ground soon became known as the area around the offices of the Mayor and the Chief Executive Officer, high up on the third floor. The first person to spot her was the caretaker, Ray Wilson. He was checking the third floor one night when he felt something touch him; turning round he saw a grey shape move into the Mayor's office. Then two women saw something in the corridor which seemed to dissolve into the wall of the lift shaft. Then the caretaker yet again, poor man, had the eerie experience of seeing lights he had turned off, blazing away.

The Council's public relations man at that time was Arthur Barker, who decided to use this to his advantage and organised a ghost-hunt at, of all times, Hallowe'en. He invited BBC journalists and the local press, plus Mrs Ann Ryan of Stockport who was something of an expert on matters psychic, plus the caretaker. They decided to try their hands at a seance, to no avail, and there was a half-hearted attempt at summoning the spirits. Nothing was seen, but when the caretaker was being interviewed live on Radio Manchester his wife, Norma, was recording it at home and the playback revealed something definitely creepy.

Cheshire: its Magic and Mystery

Stuart House, home of the Grey Lady.

In the background, behind Ray's voice, could be heard the maniacal laughter of a woman.

There is an epilogue to this tale. The building is on the site of what used to be a foundry, where metal was melted down and made into all manner of things. There is a newspaper report, dated 1857, that a woman named Margaret Hill died on these premises after being badly burned by molten metal. She had come to the building to visit her husband. Whether or not she was wearing grey at the time it is not recorded. Perhaps the maniacal laughter was hysteria after the poor person was burned.

There are many more instances of hauntings in Macclesfield but I fear that to continue with just once section of this haunted county would be tedious. There are so many more tales to relate. Many have been told and re-told – as is so often the case when a story of a good haunting comes to the public's attention – but others have never been mentioned before. It is these that I am particularly interested in for, sometimes, the oft-heard ones lose something in the translation, as it were, and the facts change in the telling. But hear a tale first-hand and it is virgin territory, matched only by the experience of actually seeing a ghost yourself. That scores ten out of ten but happens all too little. Go out with the intention of finding a ghost and a ghost will never find you; you will be avoided. Go out with an open mind and an open heart and, perhaps, a ghost may choose to make your acquaintance. Or then again, it might not ...

More Ghosts than Grains of Salt

If salt was used to keep away witches in Cheshire then it certainly did not work on ghosts in the same county. There are, it has been said, more ghosts than grains of salt in Cheshire. And that is a massive number. Every city, town, village, hamlet and every community no matter how small has its own tales to tell of ghostly goings on. Every street can, I wager, boast a ghost. Most farms in Cheshire have been the scenes of hauntings, as have its healing wells, its magical trees and its ancient burial grounds.But why should this be? Why is Cheshire not only the home of the most haunted village in the world but is, I firmly believe, the most haunted county in this land?

Tilstone Fearnall is a small hamlet on the A51 between Alpraham and Tarporley. As drivers speed along the busy road few appreciate that as they go into a dip close to Rookery Lane they are in a spot known as the Haunted Hollow. It is here that the spectre of a monk, some say ten feet in height, has been seen on many occasions. The ruins of an old priory lie nearby. The Haunted Hollow is at the rear of this picture.

The answer does not lie within these grains of salt or the sandy soil, it lies firmly embedded within the souls and the spirits of the people themselves. It is because of Cheshire people that there are so many sightings of departed spirits. These memories of those now gone are always around but it is down to people themselves to witness them. Some walk around with their eyes blinkered and others walk around with not only their eyes wide open but their minds and hearts as well. It is these who can see what others do not wish to.

Mind you, there are many mistakes made as well. And thanks to my friend Derek Hulland I can relate a number of these circumstances to illustrate the point:

It was a dark January night and the talk at Wistaston Manor had got round to ghosts. As Derek left about midnight soft, fluffy, snow was coming down and there, by the doorway, was the apparition of a monk. Derek was startled but summoned up enough courage to challenge the figure and walked towards it – only to see it was not a "monk" but a man wearing a duffle coat. If he had not gone back it would always have been the sighting of a ghostly cleric.

And then there was the 21st birthday party at The Old Vicarage, Weston, and after the sumptuous buffet the conversation got around to: "Are there any ghosts in this old building?"

There was, someone mentioned, supposed to be the ghost of an old housekeeper and others told of their own experiences of strange sightings. The evening rolled on and at about three in the morning there was a queue along the top corridor to use the bathroom. Another corridor, going off this, was not to be used because it was being renovated and therefore not safe. Suddenly, an ear-splitting scream terrorised the guests and along that corridor was what appeared to be the three foot tall figure of a struggling man. He was shouting "She's got me!" A guest had, against all advice, gone down that corridor and fallen through the floorboards.

There are many more tales of a similar nature ... . In Church Coppenhall a Mr Eardley who was a printer from Chester Bridge in Crewe was courting. He had been alarmed by reports of people seeing the figure of a ghost in the churchyard and he had to pass there on his way home. As he went by he saw a figure walking towards a grave and watched as it knelt down. He noticed it was wearing black. He felt a clout of his bowler hat and it is said he ran all the way to the centre of Crewe without stopping. When he got home he found the remains of a branch on his hat and it later transpired the Minister at the church, who had lost his wife three months previously, was of the habit of praying each night by her grave. This is what the printer had seen and had somehow managed to collide with a branch in his panic. Such stuff are ghost stories made of.

Take them with a pinch of salt if you will.

There are some who point to the Salt Trails from the Wyches and ask how many stories are told of ghosts along these ancient tracks. These trails go over to the east to Sheffield and beyond, they go south down to the City of London and they go across Wales. They were used by jaggers or packhorsemen and before then they were used by other traders. Before then they were tracks used by wild beasts who came for the precious salt. But there have, also, been many smugglers using these tracks – people who tried to evade the tax on salt and many packhorse trails have names to this day that remind us of these daring men. Smugglers Bridge in the Goyt Valley (now, unfortunately, under water because of the flooding for the reservoir) is but one. These people wished preying eyes to stay away from the routes so their comings and goings would not be witnessed. Many a tale of a phantom or a spectre has been told along these highways to scare and, therefore, to keep away.

Many a ghostly tale has been told over and over again and I do not feel it necessary to re-tell them here. The black dog of Barthomley, appearing only to foreshadow doom, is one to be investigated with other sightings of strange animals but the Combermere legend of the small girl who haunts the Abbey and whose appearance foretells the death of a member of the Cotton family has been done to death (forgive the pun). No, it is those tales that have NOT died a thousand and one deaths already in the telling that interest me. Tales like the ghost of a Roundhead or Commonwealth soldier coming through the wall at the Double Neck Swan (the Swan with Two Necks, or Nicks) in Nantwich; the spirit that moved cutlery at Churches Mansions similar to the one at Warmington Grange and Country Club. And the ghost that moved office furniture at a new business building on the road out of Nantwich towards Crewe.

Talking of Crewe, what about the phantom horseman who appears at McCracken's Corner on the Crewe to Alsager road or the spectre of a Welsh schoolmistress that has been seen at Manor Mews, Pepper Street, Nantwich? Then there's the ghost seen by the grandfather of a Barthomley man at Wybunbury Churchyard and the white dog seen at Bunbury or the ghostly form of a long-dead grandfather that appeared on a photograph taken in the Library of the Cotton family at Combermere Abbey in the 1890s. And then there are the screams that can still be heard at Farndon Bridge that are the noises made by two people who drowned there; while at Higher Walton the ghost of an old lady can be seen sitting in an armchair at Holly Hedge Farm and, nearby, strange voices are heard at Grange Mill House.

Perhaps Nantwich can rival Macclesfield for the number of hauntings it has. At the Black Lion or Drunken Duck as it is also known the landlord had to ask a ghost to "leave me alone" and it did. Then there was the case at The Old Vaults, known as The Potting Shed. This pub has cavernous cellars and has long said to be home to the ghost of a dancing bear. One section of the cellars has never had a light put in it but this dancing bear's spirit is seen there, it is said. In 1994, Mark, a sound chap from Salford had occasion to go into the cellar to check on a gas tap that had failed. He found the tap had been switched off yet he was the only member of staff in that day. How could this have happened? I'll leave the solution to you ...

There are many more well-known ones. There's the ghostly lady who haunts delightful Gawsworth Hall and the spectre of a court jester, Maggotty Johnson, is seen close to his own grave in Maggotty's Wood (I've dealt with these two before) and there's the haunting of stables at Doddington Cottage, Hunterson, near Bridgemere by a man who committed suicide after he murdered a 15 year old girl named Mary Malpas.

Bottling or Laying a Ghost

There are a number of ways of ridding oneself or one's property of a ghost, but the two most popular Cheshire ways are bottling or laying.

To explain the first method, that of bottling, perhaps I should tell a bizarre tale – albeit one that has done the rounds many times. It is a tale from Tushingham concerning the Bluebell Inn, a coaching house that can date its origins to the year 1600. The story goes that a duck was kept there, along with other animals such as hens, goats and, some tales have it, pigs as well. This particular duck must have been fed well, and might even have been fed "for the table" and it became quite a fat little animal. However, for some reason it did not find its way into the pots and pans of the Inn but was allowed to roam about freely and became something of a nuisance to the customers as it would peck their legs and ankles. So it was killed and buried under the bottom step of the cellar. The step was loosened at a later date and, the story says, the duck began to haunt the Inn, pecking at ankles and legs once again. There then followed an exorcism by twelve ministers of the church – an act not uncommon in years now gone – and these holy men prayed and prayed until the spirit of the duck was small enough to be captured in a bottle which was put into a wall and bricked up. When the Inn was renovated this century the bottle was found and, needless to say, was bricked up again.

This "bottling down" of a spirit was common enough throughout Cheshire, but I've heard it as being for a duck just this once. The twelve holy men would not all take part in the service; it was more usual for just one of the twelve to perform the exorcism. There are quite a few bottles holed up or walled up in Cheshire buildings I'll wager. I certainly know of one at a farmhouse at Wincle in the hills of East Cheshire and also one that was discovered in the wall of a house at Huntington.

This trapping of a spirit in a bottle has a parallel with the Thousand and One Nights tale of the Genie in the Bottle. There are several stories from the Middle East of spirits being captured in this way. Perhaps Alladin's Lamp is another aspect of this belief.

Another method of laying a ghost is to wait until the spectre is out and about: haunting if you like, and then a parson or priest has to lay on the spirit's grave with a Bible and a lighted candle, thereby cutting off its retreat.

But the most common method of laying is with seven or more ministers of the church – up to twelve in fact, as was the case with the phantom duck. All the priests should be armed with Bibles and lighted candles and when the ghost is spotted it should be cornered and, with candles burning, the holy men should pray "like fury". It is said the ghost will "sweal" under the prayers and if there is a holy circle round it that it cannot pass until daylight it will be "done for" or "laid". In other words, the devil will be cast out.

It has been surmised that candles are used because it has always been thought there is great virtue in the light and the belief in it probably shows a survival of the ancient sun or fire worship. Candles are still put on the altars of churches and about a corpse that is being "waked" and if something comes in the wick of a candle it is called the winding sheet and forebodes a funeral. If the

Church carries out the excommunication with bell, book and candle (as is, or was, done with those suspected of witchcraft) the candle is put out when a soul is put out of the Church.

Let us leave the many other ghosts of Cheshire at rest for now.

6

Dragons and the sleepers underfoot

As I begin writing this chapter there is a thunderstorm raging and I am hoping there will not be an electrical power failure. Gone are the days when I bashed away at an old Underwood typewriter; today it is an ultra-modern word processor and it relies on manmade energy for its power. But the earth's own powers are stronger and if they cause a break in the electricity supply then I am lost. The lightning is like the fire and brimstone of a dragon's breath and the thunder could be its roar. How apt. For it is here that we shall follow the dragon in its many guises: as a pagan monster to be defeated by the Christians, as a life-giving vein in the body of the earth and as a symbol of power.

For Cheshire not only had, and indeed, has, its own dragons. It has had its own Dragon Slayers as well. We shall look at them in a while.

The Celts, that mystical and mighty race who were, in the main, swept out of this county by the Romans (although some remained to carry on their traditions) left little or nothing in the way of words on parchment or paper, or indeed on stones. Theirs was the society that passed its secrets from father to son, mother to daughter, warrior to warrior, wise man to wise man. Our Antrobus and Comberbach Soul Gangs carry on this tradition to this day.

So what we know of their beliefs have been handed down to the present day in Groves within the mist-covered hideaways where they were safe from the Roman hordes or we have discovered artifacts that have enabled our own present-day wise men and women to piece together clues. To be quite blunt and truthful, there is one heck of a lot we do not know about these ancestors of ours. But, thankfully, there is quite a lot we do know.

We know, for instance, that this race believed our planet Earth was an entity in HER own right. She was a female. Mother Earth. And the Earth Mother was a living entity with a heart, life-giving energy flowing through her veins, a skeleton, a skin and everything else the animal body possesses. A being in her own right. And just as we have chakra points (at the top of our head, where our "third eye" is, in our throat, our abdomen, navel, just above the groin and at the base of our spine ... and some will give other points also ...) so does Mother Earth. These chakra points of the Earth are located at various locations on the globe from which major power centres are stored or emitted. The veins and arteries are the ley lines, energy lines, fairy lines or dragon lines, call them what you will, through which energy forces flow.

A good acquaintance and, I hope, a good friend of mine, Bob Trubshaw, who is editor of the Mercian Mysteries magazine, is an authority on the Omphalos, which is Greek for the "navel stone" and he has been questing the Omphalos for quite a while, with considerable success. This is the symbol of birth and where Heaven and Earth intertwine. It was the energy-giving centre that nourished the world. I have no hesitation whatsoever in recommending his work to you and know that some day he will find this spot he seeks within our land. Some have already placed it at Glastonbury and at Avebury and at other places and I have no reason to argue. The navel is but one of several spots of the earth's body – and quite a few people would have it that there is one of these on our very own doorstep. Many firmly believe that there is a chakra point within the county of Cheshire, and the Cheshire dragons, or dragon lines, hold clues to this wonderful site.

It has been said – not least by Murry Hope (*Practical Celtic Magic*, the Aquarian Press, 1987) that the "Wise Ones" time encapsulated the chakra points, sealed them and placed guardians at their entrances so that no one save those who represented The Old Ones or those who have been initiated might enter. He refers to the story of Merlin being buried beneath a stone and the energy that will be released at the right time which is represented in an esoteric fashion by the Celtic warrior King Arthur and his knights, all of them armed and with their war-horses waiting at the ready. This Celtic warrior King could, in fact, be a Romano-British warrior but if so, his descent would certainly be from the Celts and the stories surrounding him would have been handed on from the Celts. Their release could come about by energy exchange of ritual techniques or the making of the right noises, technically tonal cadences. Just as "Open Sesame" gave access to the inner world of Ali Baba and the Forty Thieves so the right words said in the right way could, perhaps, open up the spot where the knights lie in waiting.

The Celts had two forms of leaders. In times of peace they had an elderly and, therefore, wise person at the helm. Someone who was worldly-wise and who had been told many secrets that he kept. But when their enemies threatened they looked to a different leader – the warrior chief, a young, powerful and perhaps headstrong male, or female, who was skilled in the art of war. This was their Dragon Chief.

Does the tale of the warrior waiting to rescue the country in its hour of need sound familiar? I feel it will to many Cheshire people who have been brought up with the legend of Merlin and the Knights of King Arthur sleeping in readiness under that mystical escarpment known as The Edge at Alderley. It is here that I have seen the white witches prancing and it is here that more than one person is convinced they have seen the power in the form of the sleeping knights. It is here that during the second world war when Hitler's evil looked almost certain to defeat the good British that some half a dozen people who had been students together at Manchester University visited The Edge and tried to awaken the sleeping warriors with powerful prayer, some Christian some Pagan. It is here that Alan Garner, that superb writer of thought-provoking and magical words and a true son of Cheshire set a number of his books. And it is here, so a number of people believe, that one of the earth's chakra points is situated although there is also a train of thought that the energy has been lost in one way or another, either through damage to the earth by quarrying or by

Much of this has to be conjecture, purely and simply, but it is well worthy of investigation.

First and foremost, it is necessary to relate, briefly, the legend that has sprung up regarding Merlin and the Sleeping Knights. I know the majority of Cheshire people are aware of it, and I have referred to it before in Myths and Legends of East Cheshire and the Moorlands but here it is: a farmer from Mobberley crossing The Edge on his way to Macclesfield market was accosted by an old man dressed in a dark flowing gown who offered him a price for a white horse he had with him. The farmer refused and went to market but did not sell the animal and his return once again met the old man who ordered him to follow him and led the way to a rock which he struck and it opened disclosing a massive pair of iron gates at the entrance to a deep cavern. They opened and the farmer, the old man and the horse went inside and there they saw countless men asleep. Each had a milk-white steed. The old man or wizard paid for the horse and told the farmer that a day would come when these men and horses would come forth and would decide the fate of a great battle and save their country and until that date no-one would ever behold the iron gates again.

This ties in rather nicely with the story of Arthur, Rex Quondam Rexque Futurus – the Once and Future King who lies sleeping, waiting for the greatest danger ever to befall the world before he awakens again. At first the tale did not refer to Arthur, that came in a story in Blackwoods Magazine in 1839 There is documentation that says the tale was told by Parson Shrigley, former clerk and curate at Alderley who died in 1776 who had heard it from local people but only as an the man who accosted the farmer as being an "old man" and not as "Merlin".

Today, there is little or no doubt that the Arthurian legend has origins in historical fact and there was certainly a chieftain or a warrior prince of that name. He was perhaps a Christian Romano-Celt who fought the invading pagan Saxons in the early sixth century. There are also a great number of places around the British Isles claiming him as their own.

But here we must, briefly, move out of Cheshire to look at a legend that has survived in Wales concerning what happened before the legendary Arthur was born. There is a hill called Dinas Emrys near to Beddgelert where King Vortigern decided to build a castle but every night, it is said, the walls constructed that day vanished. The king called for the young Merlin who told him to drain a pool and he would find the castle's stones underneath. This was done and at the bottom of the pool there was a tent and inside it were two dragons, fighting. One was red and one was white. The red dragon beat the white and drove it away and Merlin said this signified the defeat of the invading Saxons by the native British.

Let us now return to Cheshire, and The Edge. In the thirteenth century, Ranulf the sixth earl of Chester began to build a castle on The Edge. It was a perfect spot as it looked across the entire county and any invading Welsh (they were the enemy of the Cheshire earl) would easily have been seen. The site is still known as Castle Rock and those who look carefully enough will see where the masons began their task. But hardly had the fortification been started than, for some reason, the work ceased and they decided that the other side of Cheshire would be a better spot and Beeston Castle was erected on a hill that had been occupied since the Iron Age and probably before.

Whenever a structure of such importance was to be built in those days there were only a small number of people who could decide where the best spot would be. They were the Masons, the Initiates. Their knowledge had been handed down from father to son (does that sound familiar?) and the manner in which they made the decision was a closely guarded secret. But we can surmise that one of the ways is just as the Chinese builders do to this day: the Chinese will carefully choose a spot because of the way in which the "dragon lines", as they call them, are situated. In this country we also call them "dragon" lines but we have other names for them as well: ley lines, fairy lines, earth energy lines, the list goes on. The Australian aborigines call them Song Lines, the native Americans call them Spirit Paths and they can give off powerful energy for good or for bad. The "bad vibes" occur when there has been damage to the flow and, today, dowsers refer to the damaged ones as Black Lines. Motorists call them Black Spots on roads. In 1873 E. J. Eitel wrote about the science of the Sacred Landscape in Ancient China and said it was named Feng Shui. He wrote: "There are in the earth's currents, shall I say magnetic currents, the one male, the other female, the one positive, the other negative..."

The Masons had other ways of deciding where a building should be sited; these powerful lines had to be taken into account, most certainly. And the flow of water underground was most important and it can be noticed that many of our older churches are built over underground streams, as are many pre-Christian sites such as Stonehenge. They have been given the name "Aquastats" by an authority on these matters named Guy Underwood.

So why did the Masons decide, after construction of the castle had begun on The Edge, that the work should cease?

This has happened at other places – the legends of the devil or fairies removing stones at night during the building of at least two Cheshire churches gives an unsatisfactory explanation as to why they were re-sited – and perhaps, like the story of Merlin and the Red and White Dragon, the explanation lies in the ground.

Was the construction of the castle stopped because of the disturbance to the chakra point or was the earth's energy point so disturbed by the building that it caused the work to cease? The same question in two different guises, I feel. It has been said that the earth's chakras are guarded by sleeping dragons ... both sleeping dragons or sleeping warriors could be the case at Alderley Edge.

Over the past couple of hundred years there has been much work put into the manufacture of legends of The Edge. There has been a spring there that has been venerated for centuries upon centuries by our ancestors because of its holy and healing properties and comparatively recently a carving of a wizard's face appeared upon another and it became The Wizard's Well. I think the same person or persons responsible for this were those who built a circle of stones within the woods and named them The Druid's Circle. This spot has nothing whatsoever to do with Druids. There are no energy lines going through them, they are not sited on any solar points and they are too small to be of any practical use.

What these people were doing, in fact, was perpetuating the myth and they were doing exactly the same as other people of the past. They knew there was something special about The Edge and they wanted to underline this. I think that, unfortunately, they were not aware of just why the Edge was important, although they had a suspicion or two. The same can be said of the "witches" who used to prance about there in the Sixties. They knew they were there because it was a special place but, again, they did not know what that special factor was.

The Golden Stone.

The people who did know about the enormous power The Edge contained were the same ones who utilised the power of a stone known as The Golden Stone at a spot along the track some way behind the Wizard Hotel. This stone is so named because of the energy it has given off. It is not golden in colour and it does not contain any gold but it is as precious as gold in another form. It is embedded into the ground. It is difficult to be certain now just what it was used for but there has certainly been part of it either chipped away or worn away. I think worn away. It was a stone of worship and if you take a look at the far side of it there is clearly one well-worn spot that I suspect has seen many feet placed in it over countless centuries. This then, was where a person stood upon it, but for what purpose? It was not removed to there, it is a part of the landscape and it is not there as Standing Stones are in the ground in other parts of the county and other parts of this country. Those are needles just like acupuncture needles, stuck into the body to heal and to help. It was not necessary in this case, the mystical stone was already in place upon the body of the Earth and was in the right spot. Whoever first came across this fact indeed struck gold. Out of these needles of stone (apologies to Tom Graves a worthy writer on this subject who used the phrase for the title of a book) there has been emitted a powerful energy, a golden energy. Some people, especially it appears those who make useful Mediums, are aware of auras given off by various objects such as rocks and trees and the landscape itself, not to mention auras given off by people, and a number of individuals have witnessed a gold-coloured aura from this stone. I have taken people there who have been unaware of its name and they have told me they see a golden aura. Had they been aware of its name then I would have been sceptical but I know for a fact that they were blissfully unaware of the description given to it.

But what of the Dragon Lines themselves – the Ley Lines as most call them today? They have, most certainly, been there in the past but the sad fact is that they have been disturbed. Quarrying in the mines as taken place there since before the Romans came to these shores and I know of someone who has in his possession a number of implements discovered there that had been used for quarrying and pre-date the Romans by many hundreds of years. This digging into the Earth's body has had a detrimental effect on the flow of energy through The Edge. If the Earth has a chakra point at this spot I sincerely hope it has not had a detrimental effect on this as well. Perhaps it has, perhaps it has not, but it most certainly has changed the Dragon Lines.

These straight lines of energy are often marked by sites that our ancestors venerated. Stone circles, Christian churches placed on pagan sites, wells used for healing and suchlike generally appear on these lines. It is easy to plot them on maps just by placing a ruler and seeing what lies along that straight line but it is not always accurate. The law of averages will ensure that a certain number of these sites will fall along a line that can travel for twenty miles or more and it is not definite that these lines on a piece of paper are actual lines containing energy that flows within the veins of the earth. Others find that using a pendulum over a map will find hallowed sites and it is possible to connect them in a straight line. Then that line can be called a ley line, dragon line, whatever.

The ancient stone in Prestbury churchyard.

Cheshire: its Magic and Mystery

But for me the only real way of discovering an energy line is by dowsing or divining the earth itself and following that line. If the power is there then divining rods will most certainly find that power and it is easy enough to follow a Path of the Dragon. The real fun part of this is to follow a line without knowing where it will go to and what it will go through. An elegance of undiscovered delights will unfold – the lines will go through old churches, marker stones will often be discovered and much, much more. In Cheshire alone I and others have discovered numerous ancient burial sites and stone circles that have previously been forgotten.

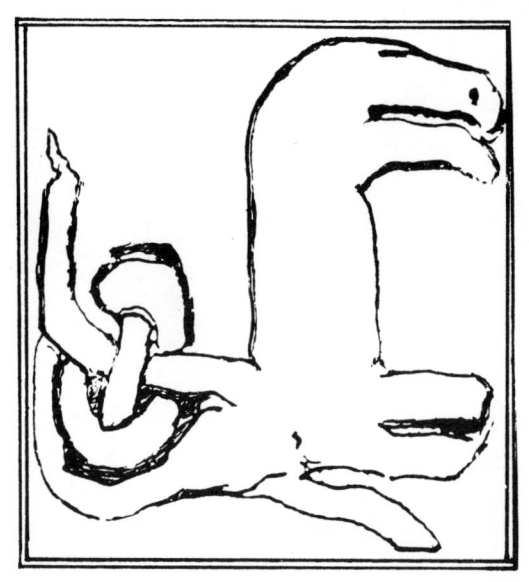

A drawing of the Dragon on the Stone at Prestbury.

Unfortunately, The Edge has lost some of the energy from within its Dragon Lines. Hopefully the energy locked within if it really is a chakra point still remains, but the quarrying has most definitely disturbed the Dragon within. And, then again, because of the amount of "black" magic that has been attempted there and because of the associations in modern day with "witchcraft" that is looked upon, rightly or wrongly, as "evil" there have been a number of attempts by well-meaning people to drive away the evil dragons and much powerful prayer has been used to banish them.

The Christian St George and St Michael, the Church's most powerful Dragon Slayers, have defeated the beast once again. Is it a coincidence that one Dragon Line goes from The Edge through Prestbury Church where a dragon is carved in a Saxon cross in the Churchyard? And is it another coincidence that one goes from The Edge through Gawsworth Church where there used to be a drawing on a wall of St George defeating a dragon and where dragon carvings around the tower point to where Dragon Lines are?

It is the traditional fate of the dragon in myth and legend to be defeated by a warrior champion fighting for good and Cheshire's dragons have most certainly been martyrs to their fate.

But perhaps we are looking in the wrong spot for our warrior, or warriors, beneath the ground.

Most of us think of The Edge as just being that area owned by the National Trust where there are nicely laid out paths through the trees and signposts to keep us on the right tracks and where there is a convenient car park, complete with handy ice cream van and toilets. Sure enough, it is, but walk across the road and there is something extremely interesting – the burial mound of, presumably, a chieftain or chieftains. The clues are not difficult to spot for the name of the place is Finlow or Fin Lowe and Lowe denotes burial mound. There in the field is a tumulus, undisturbed for probably two and a half thousand years or maybe more. One thousand metres north west of there is another burial site named Brynlow and north east of there, just on the outskirts of the present village of Alderley, there is Findlowe. Just slightly over two thousand metres in the opposite direction, south east, is Harebarrow, another name denoting a burial site – a barrow. These burial sites were not for the common or garden person, they were for the warrior chiefs or the Holy Men and if four have survived this length of time then perhaps there were even more but they have gone under the plough. They are all situated on earth energy lines; I have yet to visit one that has not been.

These burial mounds are, in my opinion, the reason for the legend of the Sleepers Under the Edge, not just because they are the resting places of obvious warriors or leaders of local tribes but because of the name given to two of them.

That name is "Fin" and we can trace this to the warrior Celts and a legendary hero of that name who was an early version of King Arthur and who is, supposedly, at rest in the Otherworld waiting for the time he is needed again. Not that these burial mounds contain Celtic people – they were made by Neolithic tribesmen who were in the vicinity quite a while before Celts – but two of them have been given the name of a legendary Celtic warrior. Just when we could never guess, but presumably during the first, second or third centuries after the birth of Christ. Or there again, perhaps much later although certainly while the memories of Celtic heroes were still very much in the minds of local people.

So who was this Fin who some people at some time must have thought lay within the burial mounds of The Edge?

Fin, or Finn, was one of the two heroes of renown of the Celts and later the Irish Celts connected him with tales of valour just like King Arthur and his Knights. He was, so the Irish stories go, named after the Fiana, a band of warriors who operated just outside of Society (as Robin Hood and his warrior band did). Finn was on a par with the other legendary hero Cu Chulainn and both were warrior leaders who protected their people, righted wrongs and had dealings with many supernatural beings from gods to monsters. Finn, however, was not connected with any tribe or clan but did have the power to see that justice was done.

This band of warriors headed by Finn was an elite bunch who had to carry out many initiations to be worthy of joining the others just as the warrior knights of Arthur had to do. They were highly educated members of the Celtic race.

Finn had a divine father and has been compared with other Celtic gods, many of whom were worshipped in the area of Alderley. The name of the River Dane or Danu tells us that the local tribe had connections with the followers of the water goddess Dana and close by on the Staffordshire border is the magic and mystical Lud Church, named after the Celtic deity Lud. This is also the site of the Green Chapel in the saga of Gawain and the Green Knight. Gawain was a Knight of Arthur and there have been tales of Robin Hood connected with Lud Church ... other echoes of past memories, I wonder? The story of the Green Knight first appears in a tale told of Finn's fellow warrior, Cu Chulainn.

Fin Lowe, the tumulus that could have given rise to the legend of the Sleepers Under the Edge.

Finn appears in Irish, Welsh and French Celtic stories and most of them tell that he did not die but lay down in the Otherworld, waiting for the time when he would be needed.

This can obviously be compared with the legend of King Arthur and his Knights asleep under The Edge. So how did the two become intertwined, if at all?

The tales of Finn the divine, according to Anne Ross who is most probably this country's foremost expert on The Celts, became stories of Finn the hero under the influence of Christianity.

Ward Rutherford in *Celtic Lore* published by Thorson's Aquarian 1993 goes further. That author says that the Knights of the Round Table and the Fianna had similar activities and came from the same cultural environment, Celtic heroic society, and suggests that one was copied from the other or they derived from a single common source. Wasn't Merlin the Magician supposedly a Celtic Druid or Wise Man?

Cheshire: its Magic and Mystery

[Hand-drawn map with the following labels:]

ALDERLEY EDGE

Holy wells

○ Findlowe Farm

× Site of beacon

● Healing Well (not in use)

BRYN LOWE ○

○ Possibly Iron Age settlement

□ WIZARD HOTEL

FIN LOWE ○

CAR PARK

F.P.

○ GOLDEN STONE

Not to scale

To Macclesfield ↓

○ HARE BARROW

SLEEPERS UNDER THE EDGE

Burial mounds & sacred sites still known.

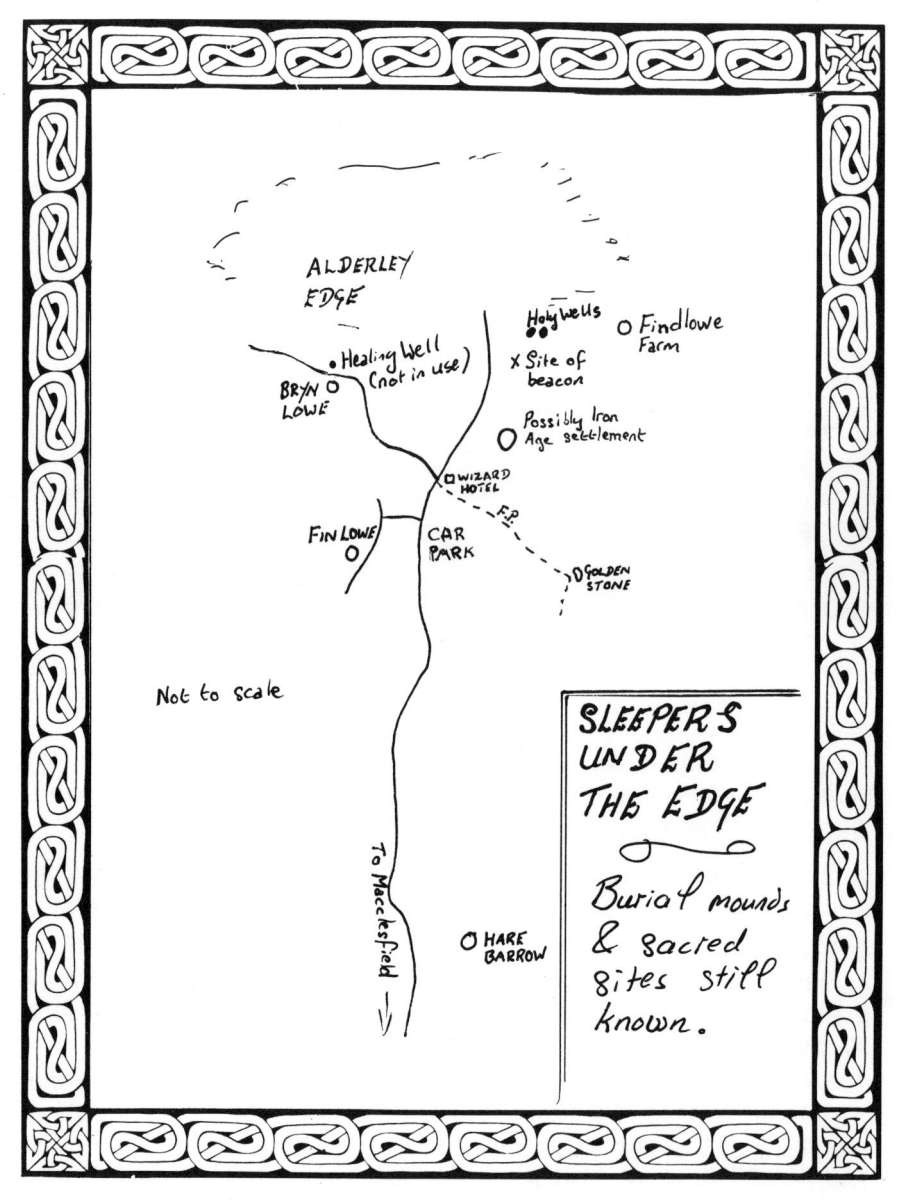

The location of the Sleepers. Hare Barrow is significant because the hare has been a creature used in divination, sorcery and in old religions. They were also connected with witchcraft. A barrow is an ancient burial mound.

Echoes of the past undoubtedly are still around The Edge. The Celtic tales of the warrior asleep and waiting for the time when he is needed later became the story of King Arthur the warrior asleep and waiting. What a coincidence it would be if Finn the Celtic Warrior who is remembered around The Edge did not spawn the legend of Arthur the Warrior under The Edge.

Surely the Sleepers Under the Edge are one and the same, Fin or Finn and Arthur? And, if that is the case, then the Edge of legends as we know it today is a fake. The real Sleepers are just over the road in the burial mound of Finn ... Fin Lowe.

Following the Dragon Paths

Perhaps here, before we take a look at Cheshire's Dragon Slayers some more, we should follow at least one of the Paths of the Dragon that are so abundant in Cheshire.

For a considerable number of years now I and others have dowsed these lines, the Dragon Paths. It is really quite simple and all you have to do is forget the mumbo jumbo that some associate with dowsing and just get down to it. All that is needed are two dowsing rods, although some people I know are capable of dowsing with just their hands – but that comes only with experience. The easiest and handiest rods can be made from one wire coat hanger cut into two L-shapes and one placed in each hand. Picture what you wish to dowse for: be it water, hidden foundations of a building or whatever. A "ley line" is rather difficult to visualise, I agree, so just set your mind to thinking that is what you are after. Then walk along the field, or whatever you are in. It is useful to have some sort of indication where a ley-line or dragon path will be and I suggest an old church or a stone circle as a near-certain spot to find one. Once one has been located the rods will both point in the direction of the flow of energy within the line. All you have to do is follow it, although there may be obstacles in your way such as housing estates or big roads or private ground. When this is so I suggest that a look at the map is called for and an attempt made to pick up the obvious line further along. And that's that. We have had some amazing adventures and delightful discoveries following these lines and I would recommend it as a harmless but fruitful pastime. I have, it must be said, attracted the wrath of a Peak Park warden or two for describing lines in other books as they seemed to think I was encouraging people to stray from the designated footpaths. I have not and am not. I make a point of emphasising that private property must be respected. This dowsing method was instrumental in discovering a stone circle right by a path that had been made by those Peak Park Rangers. I must presume they had not noticed this 3, 000 year old construction but the dowsing rods most certainly had.

But to return to Cheshire. Choose almost any church or any ancient site and I'll wager there is a dragon line there. Like the one Hilary and I followed one June afternoon in 1994:

Hobb Hill on the Dragon Line.

Our journey had taken us to Malpas where a lunchtime stop had been made and the church inspected. Yes, there were some dragon lines here all right, and one was marked by a carving of a most delightful dragon with an enchanting face. The stone was weathered and had turned a shade of green and our Green Dragon most certainly showed us the way. But this was not the line we wished to follow at that stage. That one was for another day.

We travelled westward towards Shocklach and, just by Chorlton Lane in a field at Meadows Farm there stands a tumulus – hardly recognisable as one today because of the intensive agricultural work that has taken place for centuries but nevertheless most certainly there. In fairness it must be said that the naked eye would have difficulty in spotting the saucer-shaped dome so typical of a tumulus and especially on that day for the field had just been mown. The ancient burial site is on a footpath (but, there again, the footpath is difficult to find even though a sign clearly takes you across the field). However, the divining rods found it without effort and the Dragon Path proved to be a strong one, going North North East towards Horton Green and beyond. The line went to the East of Tilston and came to Hobb Hill. This was the first indication that we were on to a good line because the name Hobb or Hob is named after the Puckish Earth Spirit Hob o'th'Hurst or Hobthrush. He has been likened to the Wood Spirit that has sprouted the name Robin and it has been thought that Hob was a real entity at one time – a friend of the fairy folk. His name also appears at ancient burial sites where Hob watches over the spirits of the departed. There are a number of houses named Hob House and, more often than not, they have been plagued with peevish poltergeist. A force to contend with indeed, and an energy easily discovered upon this line that we had begun to follow.

After going over Hobb Hill and passing the intriguingly named Lowcross Hill – had there been a standing stone or cross on that hill, marking the path, we wondered? – it went over Hook's Brook and skirted Holywell. What more of an indication did we need of a special site than that name? A Holy Well with, presumably, healing properties and, again presumably, obtaining these properties by virtue of being on a powerful Dragon Line (there's no public footpath here, the lane goes straight towards it then peters out. I think at one time it was a well-worn path to the holy well).

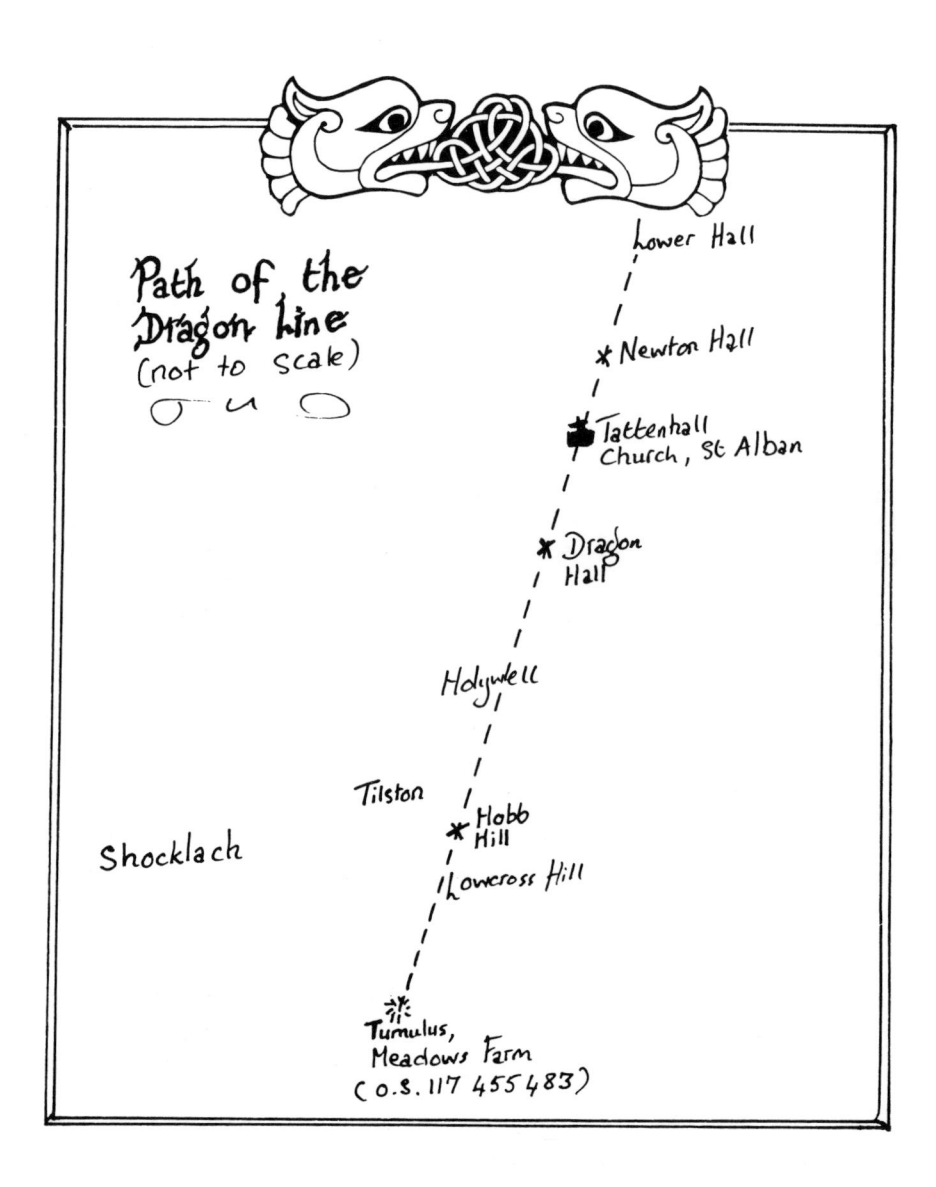

A Cheshire Dragon Line through Tattenhall.

If a pencil line is drawn on the map then the line does not go through this well. However, it should be noted that the Dragon Path is some 70 or so feet in width, and this is so very typical of these strong lines. The Path does go through the water that was once the Holy Well.

And on we went. Over the main A41 trunk road from Whitchurch to Chester where we came across a large building with an estate agent's board that advertised part of it as being for sale with planning permission for a Craft Centre or something similar.

Its name was Dragon Hall.

The signpost for Dragon Hall, obscured by the hedgerow. Is it a coincidence that Dragon Hall is on one of the most powerful earth energy lines in Cheshire?

Never had there been such confirmation. We later noticed it is there on the map under the same name (some places do have their names changed at the whim of the owners, after all) but there was no doubt as to its established name.

The line continued North North East and went directly through the Church of St Alban at Tattenhall, and it was during a brief stop there during that Saturday afternoon that some ghostly spirits were noticed and I mention these in the chapter on ghosts within this book. This could have been the end of the line we thought but it was not to be. This line had not run out yet for it went over the crossroads at Newton Hall and then to Lower Hall. This, indeed, was a Dragon Path.

Lower Hall is on another Dragon Line that starts at a tumulus at Quarry Bank south of Eddisbury Hill Fort but I will leave you to follow the tracks of these dragons for yourself if you should so desire.

As I have said, Cheshire is crisscrossed with these and part of the fun, at least as far as I am concerned, is discovering what is on these lines as you journey along them and as you pick them up again when an unpassable obstacle is reached. We did not know about Dragon Hall or the Holy Well, for instance, and would have liked to have been able to discover some more about the church at Tattenhall but, unfortunately, it was locked when we paid a visit. It is sad that so many of Cheshire's parish churches have to be locked but it is a fact of life and I cannot complain at those who see fit to protect them in this way.

So what of some others and what discoveries have been made on the ways along them? I have mentioned Gawsworth Church as not only having possessed its own Dragon Slayer, St George, on a mural now destroyed, but possessing some fine stone dragons, also, that each point the way to a Dragon Line. Some have been followed in previous works but one line that has not goes from Gawsworth Church through Astbury Church and on to a mound that could perhaps be a tumulus at Little Moreton Hall, that delightful black and white timbered building now in the ownership of the National Trust. When we visited the Hall in 1993 we had a delightful tour of the Hall and gardens and were shown the Long Gallery plus this that and the other – a guided tour I would recommend, but I did not think we had the opportunity of getting the right "feel" of the place, although this was in all probability our own fault and not any fault of the guide whatsoever who was full of all the facts and figures that most visitors wished to hear.

Little Moreton Hall, a fine building on a Dragon Line.

We were told the Hall had been built on a marsh but there was no indication as to why it had been thought necessary to erect such a wonderful building in the middle of a bog. We never expected to be told it was situated on a strong earth energy line and would have had one heck of a shock if we had been. We were told by the guide that the hillock upon which a tree now grows, and through which the Dragon Path flows, was most certainly not a tumulus. Many people had asked the guides on a number of occasions whether or not it was a tumulus and it most certainly was not as far as the custodians of the Hall were concerned. Some people say it is just a pile of earth left over from when the moat was dug and others fell it had been constructed a few centuries ago so that guests at the Hall could view the famous Knot Gardens in all their glory.

So what about these Knot Gardens?

They have also been called Serpent Gardens or Mazes or Labyrinths and were very popular in the Middle Ages and before. The fashion for them was probably brought here by the Crusaders returning from the Holy Wars. A knot is certainly a powerful weapon in itself because if a spell is cast upon someone then to tie a knot impedes that person and the act of untying that knot releases the victim from that spell. The act of marriage is known as "tying the knot" because people at wedding ceremonies tied knots to strengthen the love of the bride and groom and they were kept together. To untie these knots meant divorce. At Moreton Hall the knots are a labyrinth or maze and the symbol is one of the oldest known to civilisation but it is also a symbol that has kept many secrets. It was certainly associated with gods of the underworld and a number of churches have carvings of spirals or mazes and so do standing stones. Later many gardens were ornamented in this fashion to simply "amaze" visitors. Had our Cheshire one anything to do with the serpent within the earth or not? We may never know.

However, another interesting fact came to light just as I was concluding writing this book and I would like to share it with you. It concerns the possibility of a "mystery tunnel" and I came across reference to it in the Congleton Chronicle, a newspaper I always read with great zeal even though I have little or no connection with "Bear Town". In the weekly column "Another Week", the newspaper's well-known editor and proprietor Mr John Condliffe wrote that those who had lived in the area all their lives had always known the legend of the underground passage at Little Moreton Hall and the trouble is that, like so many other similar legends, there is not the slightest bit of evidence for it. The article mentioned that the Hall's administrator Mr Steve Adams and house steward Mrs Amanda Lunt were looking for such evidence but it must be first hand. Mrs Lunt had explained that visitors to the Hall had mentioned on frequent occasions that there existed a tunnel and many of the visitors knew someone who had been down it. The former curator, Mrs Cynthia Coulthard, confirmed that she, also, had often been told of the tunnel to the mound but had never found any evidence for its existence. Neither had Congleton History Society and both had dismissed it as "a fable". And the National Trust's archaeologist Mr Jeremy Miln had confirmed that there is not the slightest archaeological or architectural evidence to suggest such a tunnel is in existence.

The newspaper article explained that the "standard version" of the legend is that the secret passageway runs from the Hall and under the moat to reach the mound on the other side. The story adds that that is why the mound is there ... . . but some visitors have another version of the story, the article added. And that is that the tunnel runs all the way to Astbury Church, and continued "Which of course is pure nonsense and not just because of the distance involved, but also because Astbury Church doesn't have any secret entrances either, so far as we are aware."

The writer was absolutely correct, there are no secret tunnels from the Hall to the Church, via the mound, but to my way of thinking this is further proof there is something connecting them – an earth energy line, ley line or dragon line.

I have, over the years, looked at a number of legends of "secret passageways" that usually connect a church with another historical building, either a monastery, a castle or an ancient Family Seat. At Macclesfield, for instance, there has been the legend of a secret passageway going from the site of the mansion house of the Dukes of Buckingham, commonly referred to as Macclesfield Castle, and the Parish Church of St Michael and All Angels (a dragon slayer, you will notice). There is no such passage although there are a number of ancient conduits where underground streams used to feed wells and these could, perhaps, have been mistaken for passages. A number of cellars that have been discovered in very old buildings have, likewise, been referred to as parts of this mysterious tunnel. But there never has been such a construction to the best of anyone's knowledge. And, just like at Little Moreton Hall there are a number of people who say they know of others who have actually been along the tunnel. I, as the Editor of the Macclesfield newspaper for nigh on a quarter of a century, have yet to meet anyone who has, I must add – although I have certainly met and talked to people who feel they have discovered part of the tunnel under an old building or other. What there most certainly is radiating from the site of the "Castle" to the Parish Church is a strong earth energy line.

What secrets does this mound at Little Moreton Hall hold? Is it a tumulus, does it house a tunnel to Astbury Church or is it a sighting hill for the knot garden? It is certainly on an earth energy line.

Perhaps the most famous one I (and a number of others) have documented ends in Cheshire but begins in Staffordshire. Our search began in the Staffordshire town of Leek by the Parish Church of St Edward – a building famous for its mystical Double Sunset at Midsummer and for a dragon marking on a stone discovered there. The tales of a tunnel linking the church with the Cistercian Abbey of Dieulacres, founded by the Earls of Chester, are numerous and I have met an elderly lady who tells me she was taken in that tunnel by her mother and walked through it from Leek to the Abbey site. However, I have been unable to find one although a very strong energy line links the Church and Abbey and concludes at a stone circle in Rainow, north of Macclesfield.

Just one of many hundreds of legends of tunnels on earth energy lines – the Paths of the Dragon.

The Gallant Venables and St Michael

Can it be a coincidence that the Christian Slayer of Dragons, St Michael, is the name given to the Church where there is a chapel dedicated to Cheshire's most famous Dragon Slayer?

Middlewich is a nice enough little salt town and its people are even better. At one time its Church of St Michael was mother church to fifteen others that surrounded the spot. In the 1500s a chapel was built in the north aisle for the Venables family of Kinderton and it used to be surrounded by a wooden screen, now moved, that possesses twenty three family shields and on the Venables coat of arms there is a dragon with an arrow through its eye and the beast is depicted killing a child.

The story of this dragon was brought to popular notice by Egerton Leigh who wrote many romantic ballads, many of them based on popular Cheshire folklore and others based on the whims and fancies of the day. He tells of what has become known as the Dragon of Moston and relates that this dragon had three rows of sharp fangs and its "bloodshot eyes like flames did glow, its body like a serpent low, and scaled o'er as with mail." It had six claws on either side and it would tear its prey into pieces. A bear had been crushed with its tail.

The Dragon of Moston from Ballads and Legends of Cheshire by Egerton Legh, Longman and Co.,1867.

A Norman Knight, second cousin of William the Conqueror, named Sir Thomas Venables, heard of this dragon that lived in the swamp by Moston and he resolved to clear the beast or perish in the fray. The dragon seized a widow's son and the Knight came forth and shouted a challenge to the beast who, through the morning mist, heard the shouts and went towards Venables who shot an arrow into its eye and then struck its side with his sword. So loud was the shout from the dragon that warders at Beeston Castle heard it. The Knight was given land in Cheshire for this deed and the lake within the field at Moston where the dragon had resided is till known as Dragon's Lake.

So there we have it, a stirring yarn of good over evil. And an all-too familiar tale that can be associated with the Church overcoming the pagan religion. St Michael the Archangel in the Book of Revelations is the one who makes sure the way is clear for the second coming and is the Detroyer of Demons. He took over from Roman and Greek gods who were keepers of the currents of the earth such as Hermes and Mercury and he took charge of the hermits and anchorites who had been placed at special sites to watch over these natural dragon forces. They were on sites such as hill tops and sacred groves and on these places were built churches. Perhaps the Lord of the Manor was given the status of Dragon Slayer because he was Patron of the Parish dedicated to the Christian Dragon Slayer, Michael. Perhaps the Venables coat of arms depicts good over evil and the legend has grown up around this.

Or perhaps there really was a dragon ... ?

Wheelock Street, Middlewich, from an old postcard. At one time its Parish Church was Mother Church to fifteen others and it houses a memorial to Cheshire's most famous Dragon Slayer.

Meeting a Sheila-na-gig

Earlier, I had mentioned how we had visited the delightful village of Malpas and taken a tour around the Church of St Oswald. There we had come face to face with a carved stone dragon that has a cheeky grin like the Cheshire Cat and there we met a Sheila-na-gig and I stepped into a dream.

The Church of St Oswald greets you as you enter the township, for it stands proudly on a high hill. Behind this hill there is a mound, a green hill, which tradition and a bit of historical fact has it was the site of a Norman Castle. That's as maybe but energy lines going through it indicate that it has been something much more powerful – perhaps the original site of the church when worship at the site was not Christian, who knows? Perhaps this site overlooked or protected the Bad Pass that Malpas is named after? The name Malpas is derived from "malus passus" and this means bad or difficult pass. This town has long had the distinction of being approached by the worst roads in Cheshire although it is also along the Roman road linking Chester with Wroxeter. This route used to form, at one time, a much-disputed border of Cheshire and Wales.

Many assume this figure at Malpas is a monkey. It is, I believe, a mason's attempt at a Sheila-na-gig.

As we walked up to the church I noticed a hairdressers' shop across the way; nothing unusual in that you may say and you would be correct. It was an ordinary hairdressers with the salon over the top of another shop. What, for me, was rather odd was the fact that I had had a dream some time before, quite a vivid dream, in which I was in this very hairdressers. That is it: nothing more and nothing less, but I had never visited Malpas before, never mind being in that establishment but as I was having a good "nosey" through the window I realised I most certainly had visited that place in a dream. Even the chairs, the mirrors and the doors were just as I remembered them.

Anyway, that is by the way. An odd occurrence but I must say I am getting quite used to this sort of event and don't question the fact that they do happen. Entering the Twilight Zone can sometimes be perplexing but never dull.

In we went to the church and were again disappointed by the fact that the building was shut. Again I re-iterate that I appreciate the reason for this but cannot help but be saddened. What a loss, although I have subsequently spoken to others who have said they were able to visit the interior of the church. I suppose it all depends on just when the visit is made. But there was still the outside to explore and here the Masons of old had had a field-day. There were carvings of every shape and size and many caught our eyes. I was chatting to Hilary as we walked around and was telling her of a conversation I had been having with Dave Clarke, a Yorkshire folklore expert and writer on the occult, the supernatural and earth mysteries in general. We had talked of the Celtic Sheila-na-gig figures and I had mentioned that they were few and far between in Cheshire.

And then we saw her – a Sheila-na-gig if ever there was one. But just what is one of these?

To be blunt it is a fertility symbol and is a female figure in a posture that has been termed "indelicate". There are many of these figures on churches in Ireland and, to a much lesser extent, on the mainland. This is the only one I am aware of in Cheshire but I am open to being corrected on this. These figures are not something that the Church Establishment tends to brag about for they most certainly have their roots in pagan worship. Perhaps they were carved on churches to show that the old religions were not dead, just as, perhaps, the green man figures were likewise hewn. The Christian Church triumphed over the pagan followers of the Old

Religion – or did they? Were the carvers of the Sheila-na-gigs and the Green Men telling us something ? Were they saying that the Old Ways are still here? I am sure that the early Puritans and the later Victorian Puritans both destroyed many of these carvings because of this and what they depicted and represented.

But had they been carved to show the pagan (meaning "of the earth") people that although the imported religion had taken over and was all-powerful, the old religion was still alive? And did some of the Christian holy men know that this was most certainly going on and actually condoned it? Why else would they have allowed such carvings to remain around the church, for they were most certainly nothing to do with the Christian faith?

Yes, the figure at Malpas clearly shows that the old ways were followed after the Christian Church was erected there and perhaps it was not surprising in such a rural community. Even today the area relies very much on agriculture and a good few hundred years ago there would have been nothing but a rural economy and the fertility symbol would have featured strongly in the beliefs and hopes of local people. I must admit that I had expected to find a Green Man foliate head there. It felt right. And perhaps there is one that I have missed. There certainly looks as though one of the carvings outside was a foliate head but it has been destroyed either by the ravages of weather or by the ravages of people, I know not which. I intend to return to look inside the church. If you should be there before me and the building is open then please have a look and let me know what you find; I would not be surprised in the least if you came face to face with a Green Man.

Dragons of stone and wood

The interlaced dragons, perhaps a symbolic reference to the Saxons and the "British", has been found on coins minted by King Offa around 790. It is he who built the dyke separating Mercia and Wales and a carved stone found at Overchurch on The Wirral and then incorporated into the church at Upton has the interlaced dragons. If anyone should wish to see it now I am told it is in safe keeping at the Grosvenor Museum, Chester. There is also what is most probably another dragon on the same fragments and whether or not this refers to Offa or some earth energy or deity is uncertain. There is runic writing upon the stone that reads, "The community erected monument. Pray for Aethelmund". This man was a Mercian noble or ealdorman who was killed during a battle against Wessex in the year 800, it is surmised, but he is said to have owned his property in the south west of the Mercian kingdom, a long way indeed from The Wirral. Perhaps the most logical explanation is that it is another person of the same name to whom it refers.

The impressive Parish Church of Nantwich features a Dragon Slayer. The church that once housed the Knights of St John has a wonderful display of twenty stalls said to have been made from oak trees that grew at Vale Royal and carved around the year 1390. There are some weird and wonderful beasts among these carvings and underneath one of the seats is St George defeating the Dragon.

The Church dedicated to St Wilfrid at Mobberley is on a site that possessed a church before the Norman period. Excavations carried out in 1880 during restoration work unearthed traces of Saxon worship and a fine window placed at the church much later contains a depiction of St George fighting with the Dragon.

Even more interestingly, standing on a hilltop that could well have been a pre-Christian site at Great Budworth is a beautiful church that has some very strange carvings within its walls. One of them is a man with a serpent, depicting what or who we know not. Perhaps this is one of the Christian Dragon Slayers once again for most of our Christian churches are sited on Dragon Hills – hills that were sites of early pagan worship or hills that sited Dragon Lines. A fine example of this is Great Barrow near to Chester. Its very name tells all, for it was a large burial mound upon a holy site and its church now stands among trees upon a hill or holy site.

A reproduction, not to scale, of three of the dragons on stones discovered at Over Church.

Cheshire: its Magic and Mystery

A Cheshire Dragon Line

- Bunbury Church
- Spurstow Healing Well
- Hollywell (or Holy Well) House
- Pinsley Green Cross Roads
- Combermere Abbey

Not to scale

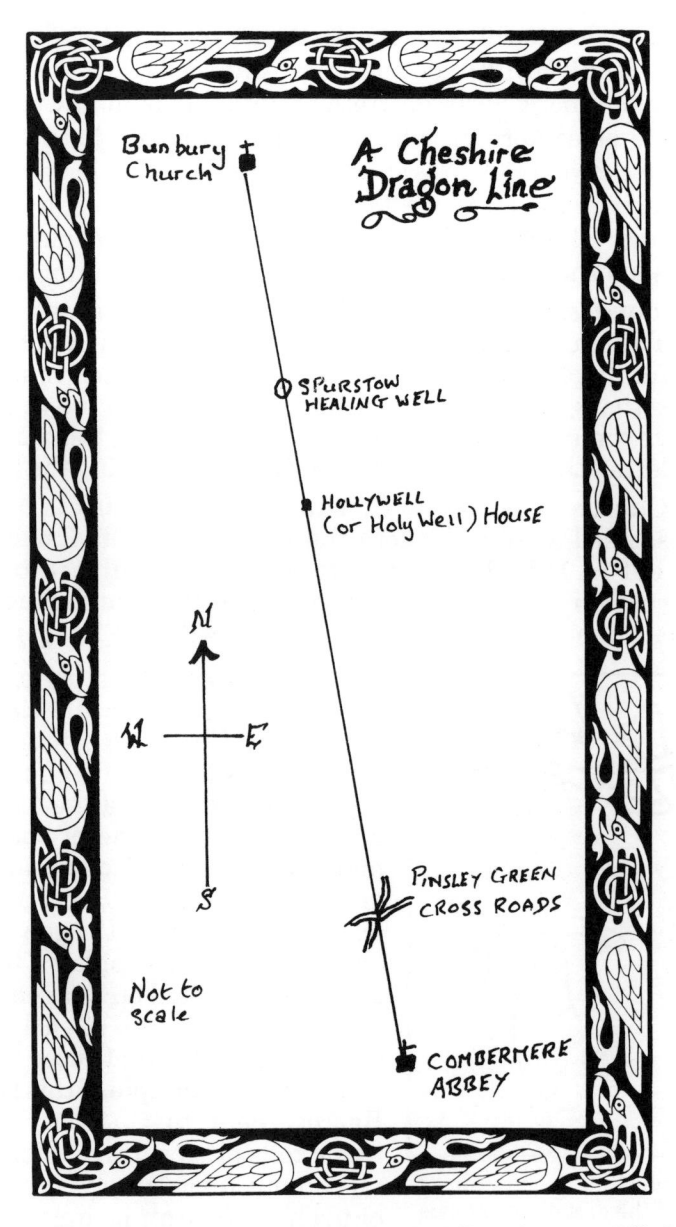

An earth energy line, ley line, dragon line, call it what you will, from Combermere Abbey to Bunbury Church.

There are many dragons under the salty earth of Cheshire and there are many more upon the hills and mounds of this county. There are memories of others carved into wood and stone within our churches showing that the Christians looked upon the energy the earth could give off as something akin to the evil beast and it had to be tamed. Or, then again, the craftsmen who depicted these beasts may well have been incorporating the natural energy within the building, unbeknown to the good people who worshipped there. What is for certain is that the Cheshire champions who slayed these dragons were worthy saints and knights of renown. The only trouble is, these beasts still remain.

Whenever a strong wind blew in Cheshire it used to be called the Dragon's Breath or the Breath of the Dragon. On October 22nd, 1913, a cyclone devastated much of the area around Beeston.

This is what remained of Castlegate Farm (J.Ennion).

The greenhouses at Peckforton Castle after the Breath of the Dragon.

7

Realm of the fairy folk

February is not the best of months to climb to the top of Toot Hill, a prominent grassy spot perched above Macclesfield Forest. At the best of times it is windswept and, at the worst, is akin to the Mountains of the Moon – desolate, wild and unwelcoming. But that particular day was different. It was a rare February day when the sun was shining as best it could and there was little or no wind. There had been a frost that morning and there was the promise of more that evening but, all in all, the day was a good one. Several hours of daylight lay ahead and so Hilary and I set forth for Toot Hill.

I have visited that spot on many occasions and have always found it something rather special. The views alone are worth the trek (but please, please note it is on private land) and perhaps because there are uninterrupted views of Derbyshire, Cheshire and Staffordshire from the top our forefathers decided to build a hill fort there. At least it is thought that was what it was but, to be blunt, no-one really knows for sure. There is still much evidence of fortification or something similar to be seen there (see Magic, Myth and Memories book) and perhaps one day someone will decide just what it was.

But that is not why Hilary and I decided to visit that particular site on that particular day. There was no reason other than we both decided that we should; and that has always been the best of reasons as far as we are concerned.

So off we went. Up to the hill that we later decided should be called a Fairy Hill.

Our journey took us along the edge of a drystone wall and as we plodded up to the summit sheep wearing their winter wool chewed the grass and stared at us. We must have been the first people they had seen for many a day except the farmer who would, no doubt, bring them extra winter rations. Perhaps they were wondering whether we were bringing them food but would not venture near enough to find out. It was then that Hilary first saw the hare. A large, floppy-eared creature darting here and there in front of us and an unusual sight for that winter's day. Next month its mad antics would not be unusual at all but it was a rarity indeed for February.

Whenever Hilary sets eyes on a hare she always thinks it is an omen of good luck and she knows something nice will happen that day; so she was delighted at what was happening. I wanted to carry on towards the summit where the mounds of earth hold many secrets and I was hoping that, perhaps, Hilary's psychic ability would throw some light on the mystery of Toot Hill but she wasn't having any of this. She wanted to follow the hare – and who am I to argue? The creature bobbed hither and thither, sometimes going out of sight but always popping up again and darting, zigzag, across our path. Off we went to the side of the hill and away the hare lobbed towards the plantation of fir trees further away. And we followed. It disappeared again then re-appeared behind a tuft of grass and we followed. Then we lost it again and, this time, waited for a considerable while for it to re-appear but to no avail. It had gone. So just what was the point of following it, I wondered? We were quite a way from where we had originally intended and the whole exercise seemed fruitless.

Then Hilary spotted the hare again. It was standing on its hind legs, its head reaching upwards and its two front legs seemed to beckon us. Imagination, of course, but the animal itself was not being imagined – and neither was the tumulus, an ancient burial mound, on which it was standing. And on that burial mound right by the hare was a stone, some three feet or a metre in height. A tombstone if you like, marking the spot where an ancestor of some two thousand plus years ago was lying undisturbed. We walked towards it and the hare did not move until we were but a stone's throw away and then it darted off, not to be seen again that day.

We went up to the tumulus and paid our respects to the person who lay beneath and noticed that around the stone that marked the top of the mound there was a circle of grass that was both a different texture and a different colour to the rest of the grass around that site. Throughout Cheshire this sort of grass ring is known as a Fairy Ring and is where fairies are said to hold their dances. There is also the belief in this county that if anyone was to run nine times round a fairy ring when there was a full moon then it was possible to hear the little people talking and laughing. The tradition goes further, for it is supposed to be unwise to sit on such a ring at May Eve, Midsummer's Eve or All Hallow's Eve because at those times you can be spirited away by the fairies. As it was not a full moon we did not see the necessity to run the circle nine times and as it was not one of the other three dates we felt safe enough.

Cheshire is an agricultural county and it is unusual for such a county to have many tumuli because they would, in all probability, have gone under the plough many years ago. This has most certainly been the case up and down Cheshire but there are quite a few still intact across the Cheshire Plain and even more in the hills where the land is not so easily ploughed and is given over more to sheep than the plough. But, there are still quite a few about and many of these are known to Cheshire people as Fairy Hills. In some instances, like at Somerford Booths near Congleton, it is noticeable that the burial mound has not been ploughed but could very easily have been; it is in the middle of a field and has been deliberately avoided. Perhaps this is because there is also the belief that ill-luck will befall anyone who disturbs such a site ... either because it is a burial place of the dead or it is the abode of the fairies.

Around the Toot Hill area, in Macclesfield Forest, local people certainly believed in fairies and there survives to this day a belief that before a field is ploughed or harvested then food must be left out for them. I once was shown a tiny pipe no bigger than a farthing piece that was found at Kettleshulme and was said to be a fairy pipe and near to Croker Hill where the communications tower now stands there is a place called Fairyhough. There is also a "Fairy Glen" just to the south of there.

In 1991, I had the pleasure of being invited to a farmhouse near to Wincle and was told by the occupant, who, unfortunately, is now no longer with us, that she had most certainly seen a fairy. I asked her to explain and she said that when she was some six or seven years old (she would have been in her eighties when I saw her) she and two friends had gone to a field adjacent to the River Dane to pick mushrooms. It was early morning and as they were scooping up the fresh field fungi one of them shouted to the others and they ran over to her. She told them to duck down and this they did without question and she pointed to a hillock on which there was a fairy ring or a circle of grass different from the surrounding grass. The friend told the other girls that she had seen a fairy there and they, not surprisingly, did not believe her and started to laugh at her but she was adamant and no amount of teasing by her companions would make her change her story.

I have, I'm pleased to say, a tape recording of the lady relating what happened next (I am not mentioning her name because she asked me not to as she was a devout churchgoer and, even though she has now passed on, her family are still very much in evidence in the area).

This is what she said:

"We were waiting around for the best part of fifteen minutes and were getting pretty restless by then but May (the girl who had spotted the fairy) kept telling us to hold back and wait and see if we could see anything again. We looked and we looked but we suspected she was a-kidding us because we could see nothing and neither could she. I was for off and so was Betty (the other girl) but she kept telling us to wait and we did. But then I'd had enough and got up to walk away and get some more mushrooms and Betty shouted 'Look!' I turned round and the two of them were pointing to the little hill and I looked and saw something, I couldn't say what. They were saying it was a fairy but I wondered whether it was a bird, a thrush or something, in the grass. There was something there all right but I looked but couldn't make it out. May was saying 'It's a fairy' and I looked and looked. She said it was wearing brown and I looked some more and saw something moving. It wasn't a bird and it wasn't an animal. I don't know. They were both saying it was a fairy. It looked the size of a thrush and was moving about in the grass but I don't know."

Deva the water nymph or goddess depicted as a fairy with her attendants during the 1910 Chester Historical Pageant.

There is a long pause on the tape at this point because the lady went into what I can only describe as deep thought, as though she was trying to recollect the events of that morning, or as though she was wondering whether she should continue. I am not sure which. I asked her if she was all right and would she like a drink (she had made a pot of tea but it was still brewing under the tea cosy in front of her coal fire) and she said she would. I poured.

After a while she began to speak again: "I thought they were kidding me still. They kept saying, in loud voices, that it was a fairy and I told them to hush because they'd frighten it away. I thought it was a bird, a thrush. I could see some speckles and a thrush has them on his chest. One of them, I can't remember, said he was carrying a bag and I looked. There was something and I screwed my eyes to try and look more. It had stopped moving and it looked like a person, a tiny one. I looked. It did look like a little person, it did. It was like looking at a book, at a picture in a book, a children's book. It didn't move and I think it had heard us 'cos we were all chattering. It's a wonder we hadn't frightened it off, three girls giving it all about this fairy. I thought it was a fairy then. I looked and looked and May said we should go up to it, it was about as far that clock away (about ten feet or three metres) and didn't move; I think it was scared. May got up and ran towards it and it scampered off down the hill to the Dane. It was like a mouse then how it ran, scampering like, like mice. It wasn't a mouse though, it was like a little man in a brown suit, no, not a suit, but brown top and trousers, like a jerkin on the top and brown. It was a little man. A fairy like. I'd never seen such a thing and we all of us ran down the hill after it and I shouted to stop in case we trod on it and we all stopped and looked round but we couldn't see it. That was all, because we couldn't find it, it had gone. It wasn't there. But it was a fairy."

She drank her tea. Then she said: "May wanted to tell her mother but her mother was Chapel and I said 'Don't' as she wouldn't believe it. Them as are Chapel don't. And Betty said don't tell anyone, it was ours, so we didn't but then May was telling everyone at school and I was frightened that someone would tell teacher but they didn't. I'm pleased."

The old lady drew a picture of what she saw and it was a picture of a man.

"Did it have wings?" I asked.

"I don't know" she said. "I didn't see any, but May said she saw a bag over his shoulder. It was definitely wearing brown and had a waistcoat, that's why I thought its chest was like a thrush. It was a waistcoat."

Shutlingslowe, not Shutlingsloe as the Ordnance Survey would have it, and to the right on the horizon can be seen a tumulus, known in Cheshire as a fairy hill.

Carrying the Stones

At Ince, on the Cheshire bank of the Mersey, the church of St James stand proud and true and this church is associated with the fairy people.

The church is on the site of what once was a Norman chapel and the Rev. F.G. Slater, M.A. recorded a local legend that the original builders of the church wanted it to be in the northern part of the village of Ince but the fairies did not approve of its siting and each night they carried the stones away to the opposite end of the village.

Wartime and post-war radio personality Wilfred Pickles chats with 82 year old Ned Wood of New Lane Farm, Prestbury, on May 6th, 1954. Ned knew much local folklore and told Wilfred that he knew of a "fairy mound" in the vicinity.

This continued for a considerable time until the builders gave up and decided they could not beat the fairies and allowed the church to be built where it now stands. All well and good, but this sounds remarkably like the legend at Over where it was the devil who carried the church to where he wanted it, and also the church of St Lawrence at Stoak and at Ince.

There is a similar legend at Bramall Hall, that remarkable black and white building close to sprawling Stockport. There are earthworks (Fairy Hills?) a half a mile to the south of the present Hall and it is here that local tradition has it that the Hall was originally intended to be built. It is also a spot known as Fairy Wood or Crow Holt Wood. In 1880 a historian named Alfred Burton wrote of the earthworks:

"On the summit of the rising ground to the south of the hall (and which is of the highest ground in the township, affording a fine view of the surrounding country) are the remains of the first hall erected by the Bromhales. The spot is now covered with a fine plantation and is known as Fairy Wood, the legend being that as fast as the builders laid the stones and the timbers in the daytime the fairies removed them in the night to the present spot, till the owner, tired of his fruitless struggle, abandoned the spot and erected the hall in its present position".

In 1909, Frederick Moorhouse wrote that these "earthworks" had once been a deerhay into which animals were driven for killing and for sorting.

The story of the church, or in the Bramhall case, a Hall, being removed in the night appears up and down the country.

At Over there is the long – told story that the church of St Chad once stood in Over Square but the Devil in this case carried it off in its entirety, complete with foundations, soon after it had been bestowed upon the Abbot of Vale Royal Abbey during the reign of Edward 1 but the monks remembered that he was supposed to be scared by loud noise so they rang the Abbey bells as loudly as they could and the devil dropped the church and it floated safely to the ground landing where we find it today. The tale of the devil moving the church is told at Stoak as well. But why, at Stoak and Over and at other spots, should the devil have been substituted for fairy people because, after all, they were not supposed to be in league with him? Strange indeed, but there is a theory that fairies were, in fact, real people but people who were outcasts, or people who lived away from civilisation – pagans who were direct descendants of Neolithic man and lived away from "modern" man through choice. These fairy folk were, therefore, anti-Church and anti-Christ it was surmised and, as such, were of the devil. Perhaps this is why the "fairies" were blamed. There was certainly a "Fairy Hill" around Ince on which some holy men built their own church, perhaps to defeat the pagan dragon therein. The site of the tumulus or burial mound was where Stanlowe Abbey was later built. The name Stanlowe denotes Stan – a stone, and Lowe – a burial mound.

A depiction of the legend of Over Church.

Perhaps it was these outcasts who did not want anything to be built on their own precious sites who removed the stones, who knows?

I have delved much more into this theory of fairies being an outcast race in my book *Staffordshire: its Magic and Mystery* and in that work I take a look at a long-lost village on top of Bosley Cloud that stands astride the Cheshire and Staffordshire border and from where, so some say, a race of people came. These were, it is believed, the fairy folk of our myths and legends. I will leave you to decide.

Throughout Cheshire the white thorn has been associated with fairies. It is said that this tree attracts the little people and that it is also a holy tree. A number of stone crosses in villages throughout the county were associated with the white thorn and many had thorn trees growing either alongside or on top of them – at Eaton, near Chester, and Alderley for example. There is also a tradition that the fairies dance around these stone crosses; Mottram St Andrew and Gawsworth both have this legend and at Lymm, where its cross is carved out of the very stone that Lymm is built upon, the tradition also survives.

In times now gone there was a great respect for those places that had earth power in the form of dragon or fairy lines and those spots that were also gentle, calm, quiet and restful places upon Mother Earth. Such were the hideaway fairy dells where these mystical folk could make themselves known to the humans. These spots were plentiful and there are still some to be found if we but seek. And such were the spots that became places of worship where, later, stones would be erected as totems to honour the Spirit of the Place. Round these stones, or crosses as we laughingly call them today, the fairy folk would manifest themselves. There are some who say they still do. I have spoken to a few in various parts of Cheshire who believe this. I have spoken to a farmer at Antrobus who told me that he has seen them dancing in a dell. He and some of his fellow National Farmers Union members still put out a saucer of milk for them (perhaps the fairy folk disguise themselves in the form of a hedgehog when they come for this milk?).

The hedgehog is sometimes known as the pig to Gypsy folk, the Romanies. These proud people have dwindled over the years and the travellers along our lanes are now going to Stonehenge to battle with the police or are wandering tradespeople who move from derelict site to derelict site and are not the true Romanies. They are not the travellers Cheshire people knew of earlier this century who were fine horsemen and who knew the lore of the land and the lie of the land better than any. They knew which herbs were suited for what and they knew how to talk to animals. They also talked to the fairy folk, it has been said.

I was very pleased when Macclesfield Borough Council decided to renovate the delightful caravan that stood outside the Library and the former Wilmslow Urban District Council Offices for many a year. This was Romany's Caravan, the one used by Bramwell Evans the writer and broadcaster whose pen name was Romany and it had been vandalised and left to rot away. How well I remember looking at that caravan when I used to go to the meetings of Wilmslow Council as a young reporter to cover the proceedings for the Wilmslow Advertiser newspaper and I used to envy the lifestyle of the open road led by Romany. I could almost smell the camp fire and the food cooking over it.

G.R. Mannion, writing in the *Macclesfield Courier* as far back as 1812 (a year after that newspaper was founded) told his readers about the people he named the Cheshire Gypsies. First of all he launched into fanciful ideas about how these people had come to our shores from Egypt and were the Lost Tribe of Israel and then he told of some of their traditions, beliefs and ways. He was the grandson of a Romany he said, and some of his family were then still travelling the Cheshire lanes. Surprisingly, they kept within the county boundary for they looked upon their domain as Cheshire and only Cheshire. They would not cross into Shropshire or into Staffordshire or Lancashire or across to Wales. They were Cheshire and only Cheshire.

He told how they cooked the hedgehog wrapped up in clay and when the fires had baked the clay it was removed and off came the spines with it. It tasted, he said, like pork. But before they would eat their "pig" they would give leave some on a plate for the fairies; they always left a seat vacant in case one should visit them.

One of the groups, or "tribes" as he referred to them, had as their head an elderly lady known as Mother. In fact, all the Cheshire tribes were headed by a "Mother" he said. This particular one could speak the fairy tongue he claimed. It was a mixture of what he termed "Old English" and Welsh (perhaps he was describing a form of Celtic, who knows?)

    Mother was the one who could always be relied upon to see these people and she was often prone to talking to them although others about her could see nothing; but they knew they were there if Mother was talking to them in this strange tongue. And there has been more than one occasion when a horse in foal would produce milk and before its offspring could drink from its mother, some had to be given to the fairies. They always had the first pick. Whether or not he had seen one himself we are not told and we are not told how they looked to the Mother Gypsy or her tribe but he did feel that the Romanies had fairy blood in them. Perhaps this could tie in with the theory of the "outcasts" who did not mix with the "civilised" humans and perhaps I may be forgiven for referring you to the chapter on the Fairy Folk of Biddulph Moor that I look at in my book on Staffordshire for I feel the two have a lot in common.

Nomansheath near to Chester. Many areas throughout the country that were close to boundaries were known as No Man's Heaths, for they were neither owned nor claimed by anyone. These areas were usually heathland that was of little agricultural value. It is from this we get the term "Heathens", being people of the Heath. Nomansheath was a favourite spot for the travelling people of old.

8

Grinning cats, black dogs and panthers

Thanks mainly to that son of Daresbury who called himself Lewis Carroll, the county of Cheshire has become synonymous with a grinning animal now known as the Cheshire Cat. Few are unfamiliar with the surreal tale of Alice's Adventures in Wonderland in which the creature disappears, except for its grin.

But what is, or was, a Cheshire Cat?

Lewis Carroll or Charles Lutwidge Dodgson was not the first to write about this animal. That prize must be awarded to John Walcot, M. D., writing under the pen name Peter Pindar between 1794 and 1801 when he penned: "Lo! like a Cheshire cat our court will grin." Not much of a clue there, so perhaps it has been a verbal tradition in Cheshire, and that would account for the lack of words written. Not so, it appears. It has never been a very common saying within this county and the first attempts to actually track down its origins came in 1851 when a letter appeared in a book entitled *Notes and Queries* which asked: "Will some of your correspondents explain the origin of the phrase 'Grinning like a Cheshire Cat?' One ingenious theory – that Cheshire is a County Palatine and that the cats, when they think of it, are so tickled that they can't help grinning – is not quite satisfactory. This refers to a letter of Charles Lamb the famous essayist, who wrote: "I made a pun the other day and palmed it upon Holcroft who grinned like a Cheshire Cat (Why do cats grin in Cheshire? Because it was once a County Palatine and the cats cannot help laughing when they think of it, though I see no great joke in it)".

Answers given to *Notes and Queries* were: "I remember to have heard many years ago that it owes its origin to the unhappy attempts of a sign painter of that county to represent a lion rampant, which was the crest of an influential family, on the sign boards of many of the inns. The resemblance of these lions to cats caused them to be generally called by the more ignoble name."

This influential family was the Egertons, by the way.

The same idea prevailed in the following reply: "Both the lion and the leopard where they occur in sign board art were vulgarly spoken of as the Cat. The Blue Lion, for instance, was the Blue Cat. Now the City of Chester impales for its arms the Lions of England with the arms of the Earls of Chester, the lion ... should be described as a leopard, some say. It is this full-faced attitude of the leopard that probably suggests the grinning attitude because the mouth of the lion, or leopard, is generally represented by heraldic carvers and artists with a curve upwards to each extremity."

Robert Holland in *Lancashire and Cheshire Antiquarian Notes* suggests: "it is just possible that the arms of the Earls of Chester, namely a wolf's head, may be the original Cheshire Cat, for I am bound to say that in the engraving of the coat of arms of Hugh Lupus, as given by Sir Peter Leycester, the wolf's head might be very well mistaken for that part of a cat; while the grin is unmistakable."

The Cheshire Cat from *Alice in Wonderland*.

Another correspondent said: "Some years since Cheshire Cheeses were sold in this form moulded into the shape of a cat, bristles being inserted to represent the whiskers. This may possibly have originated the saying."

This is highly unlikely for Cheshire cheese was the high class cheese of Britain and would not have been vulgarised and thus had its value reduced. It sold well enough without a gimmick.

A writer in *Stockport Notes and Queries* said it should be "To grin like a Cheshire polecat" as these animals were larger and more fierce-looking than ordinary cats.

Egerton Leigh, who wrote much about Cheshire folklore, said: "One needs not go far to account for a Cheshire cat grinning. A cat's paradise must naturally be placed in a county like Cheshire, flowing with milk."

Variations of the saying have been quoted as "To grin like a Cheshire cat eating cheese" and "To grin like a Cheshire cat eating green gravel".

But none of these writers have allowed for one thing. The Pott Shrigley Cheshire Cat.

At Christopher's Church at Pott Shrigley stands beside one of the oldest trading routes in these islands and salt from Cheshire went by this trail for hundreds, if not thousands, of years, across to Yorkshire and perhaps then across the sea. This hamlet just north of Bollington possesses what is probably the last working gas street lamp in the country and it also possesses the finest example of a Cheshire Cat within the county. In affect it has two examples but one is not as magnificent as the other. One of the carvings on the exterior is a grinning Cheshire Cat and there is also the head of what could probably be the Queen of Hearts. Inside the church there is, underneath the chancel arch, a stone face of a Cheshire Cat, grinning from ear to ear. I have asked the question in *Magic, Myth and Memories* whether this is where the writer of *Alice in Wonderland* received inspiration to write of, and picture, the Cheshire Cat. His father was a Cheshire clergyman and they had relatives in Cheshire so it is, perhaps, possible that he visited Pott Shrigley.

If not, then there is still the question of what is the Cheshire Cat. Again, I have mentioned before that in my opinion, it denotes the "Cheshire Grin" of the felon's cut throat, grinning from ear to ear. The power of life and death was granted to the Foresters of Cheshire and one of the ways they ridded the land of poachers was to cut their throats or garotte them – hence, the "grin" of the cut from ear to ear. Look how the Cheshire Cat has no neck and its grin is from ear to ear. The Foresters within Pott Shrigley were the Davenports and their coat of arms shows a decapitated felon. And the body of the sacrificial victim found in the peat at Lindow Common and identified as a Celtic prince or suchlike had been garrotted – the Cheshire Grin or Smile again.

Just before we leave the realm of the cat, we must travel over to the Wirral. On Bidston Hill, close by the Observatory, there are a number of carvings in the stone and they are thought to date from around the second century, AD. They are, I think, Celtic in origin. One of the carvings is given the name of Moon Goddess, for she has a moon at her feet but, more importantly, she has the face of a cat. Over at Timbersbrook underneath The Cloud there is a group of rocks known as the Cat Stones where, it is said, people used to worship the "Cat Goddess." Could the Moon Goddess and Cat Goddess be one in the same – a Celtic deity worshipped in Cheshire – the Cheshire Cat?

From cats to dogs

I have a friend, an architect of international renown, who owns an oil painting. It is rather a surreal work depicting a tormented person with a black dog draped upon his shoulder. One day I asked him what the painting represented .

"That's my black dog." he said.

I asked him what he meant, because I knew he had no pets.

"Whenever I am in a dark or sullen mood, or in a rotten bad temper then I've got a black dog on my shoulder. That's the black dog."

How many of us have a similar black dog upon our shoulders, I wonder. I know I do. Why should the creature be a dog and not some other animal?

And why does Cheshire possess stories of black dogs haunting people or places and foretelling doom?

Perhaps we need to go back quite a long time to get to the root of the matter; back as far as the time of the Pharaohs for it was they and their Priests who believed the dog-headed god Anubis guided the souls of the dead to the Underworld. This animal has also been worshipped by other ancient civilisations, namely Babylon and Assyria. The Egyptians worshipped and cherished dogs so it was hardly surprising that the Hebrews felt just the opposite about these creatures. They would have no truck with the belief that dogs could guide people to the next life and that dogs could communicate with the spirits.

For much the same reason the followers of Islam dislike dogs but the Persians believed that a dog guarded the bridge to the next life and there is a story that it barks so fiercely that the Devil is driven out of the souls of those who walk across the bridge into the next life. The Buddha returned as a dog to bring enlightenment.

Patricia Dale Green who wrote *Dog* (Hart-Davis 1966) says that there is the image of the personal dog-ghost that protects people on lonely roads and, as we have seen, the divine dog that protects souls on their way to Heaven and the dog has been depicted as receiving the souls of dying people. It has, she wrote, also judged souls after death.

With this in mind it is no surprise that certain Black Dogs in Cheshire have been connected with the spirits of the departed and also with those about to die.

One of the most famous is the Black Dog of Barthomley. This one is said to haunt the area around the Church and the Rectory and its appearance foreshadows the demise of the Rector of the Parish. The fact that this spirit animal appears around the vicinity of the church brings to mind the tradition that is prevalent throughout the British Isles that the spirit of a black dog guards churchyards from both witches and the Devil himself. According to Katharine Briggs in her superb *Dictionary of Fairies* (Allen Lane 1976) this creature is often referred to as Church Grim and those who saw it generally took it as a death warning. She refers to Ruth Tongue's Forgotten *Folk Tales of the English Counties* (Routledge and Kegan Paul, 1970) in which she writes that when a new churchyard was opened the traditional belief was that the first person to be buried there had to guard it against the Devil. In order to save the soul of a human having to do this task a pure black dog was buried in the north part of the church yard as a substitute.

Across the county at Godley Green there has sometimes been seen a huge hound said to be, at least, as large as a cow with huge eyes and a foaming mouth, like a rabid canine. Near to the church at Bunbury there has been seen on several occasions a white hound with a chain around its neck. Near to the spot there has been seen the spectres of a horse and rider. Whether the white dog has the same connotations as the black one it is difficult to say. Perhaps there is nothing to connect the two but the fact they are dog spirits.

The Black Greyhound Smithy named after the pub, now a house, across the road. A black greyhound is reputed to have foreshadowed doom for the Stanley family.

And at Over Alderley, there is a building that is today quite a landmark. It is the Black Greyhound, built in 1910 as a smithy across the road from where a pub of that name used to be and is now a house. The public house was closed along with other public houses on the Alderley Estate of the Stanleys some time ago, but whilst it was an ale house it went under the sign of the Black Greyhound. The Stanleys of Alderley Park were, in the main, delighted by local superstitions and folklore. Various members of the family have chronicled them and they have fitted some for their own entertainment. A gardener of Alderley Park was said to have mentioned the sighting of a black greyhound was an ill-omen for the family. And, still on the subject of black dogs, the Cathedral at Chester has been said to be haunted by such an animal. This is not one of the oft-chronicled tales and I only came across it by accident, while reading through copies of the Chester Chronicle many years ago. The spirit animal is said to walk by the north door of the Cathedral. This door is, in some religious buildings, known as the Devil's Door.

There is the often-told tale of the werewolf of Longdendale said to have very much alive during the reign of Henry II. The Abbot of Basingwerke was asked by local people for help against this creature and so, in the best traditions, he cursed it so that it should remain in whatever state or condition it was at the time. The legend then says that King Henry and Prince Henry his son plus local dignitaries like the Lord of Longdendale and the Baron of Ashton went in pursuit. The Prince was separated from the others and the werewolf attacked him. A ferocious fight ensued and there was much give and take but eventually the Prince began to lose his strength and, in the nick of time, the Baron of Ashton appeared and killed the beast. The body was cut open and three heads of babies it had eaten that day were in its stomach. Later it was learned that a forester had seen the werewolf in the forest and it was screaming and trying to tear off its own skin. The scream was that of a woman. A good tale made better by repeated telling and interesting in that it made out the monarch and his son, plus local barons to be the heroes. I think it was not a tale manufactured by the common man but by someone who wished to put the hierarchy in a good light.

And finally we must look at the trail of a panther and a ghostly building...

In the very depths of rural Cheshire, in the Dane Valley, there was a Tudor or Stuart building known as The Dumkins. In the 1970s the building became so dilapidated that it had to be pulled down and, I am pleased to say, the beams, roofing stone and stones were preserved with the intention of re-erecting it somewhere else at some later date. One suggested site was the visitors' centre in Macclesfield Forest near Langley Reservoirs. At the time of writing this nothing has happened and I wonder whether memories are failing and an anonymous pile of rubble in some Council yard somewhere is being lost. I sincerely hope not.

The Dumkins, a medieval farmstead now demolished, map reference SJ 948647. This spot is said to be haunted and the paw mark of a huge cat-like creature has been found close by (M.Winnell).

The 17th century farmhouse was colloquially named The Dumkins and stood above Barleyford Farm, Dane Valley. The timber-framed wattle and daub farm was long said to be haunted and the site where it stood still possesses a spirit or two, I am told. It is around here that Hilary and I have witnessed the wonderful sight of a red deer strolling, unconcerned, among the fields and woods and then springing over a drystone wall. It is here that an ancient track runs towards Chester from Wincle Grange – an ancient route that has worn its way about six feet into the ground because of constant use but is now almost forgotten.

And it is here that footprints of a giant cat or possibly a panther have been seen by a local farmer. That is it: nothing more and nothing less. There has not, to my knowledge, been a sighting of a big cat and no animals have been taken in strange circumstances to my knowledge. However, the farmer is adamant the tracks were that of a huge cat. This got me to thinking about something that happened several years ago ... I was signing copies of a book at W. H. Smiths in Macclesfield and a gentleman purchased a copy and got into conversation with me. He said that he and his wife had been sitting in their car at Wincle, which is very close to The Dumkins, drinking a flask of coffee. They saw what they thought at first was a huge black cat but it was far too big to be a domesticated one. It was, they think, a panther.

9

Magic water, mysterious stones

Cheshire is a mysterious county. In many ways it is an enigma. It has a history as old as time yet it hides away the proof of this. There are few stone monoliths to tell us that early man worshipped within the county but he most certainly did. Straddling the border of Cheshire and Staffordshire we have the prehistoric Bridestones, or all that is left of them, and just down the way on Bosley Cloud there are a few carvings that, in all probability, were etched by our predecessors. There are a few more worthy of examination. The Bowstones on the moors of the East above Macclesfield possess power, even today, that would have been used by men of old and these high hills contain one or two more stone pillars that we may look at.

There are also a number of rocks, boulders, stones, call them whatever, tucked away across the Plain – and the Wirral possesses a township that traces its mystic stone to Thor, the god of thunder.

But the worship of holy, healing, water is now far more in evidence throughout the county than the worship of stones. However, tied in with the worship of water and the deities that were thought to exist within these waters there are some stones, either carved into troughs or out of the rock faces or into the rocky ground, that possess a quality that is still there if the seeker wishes to find.

Within this chapter I have tied in both stones and water under one banner for I firmly believe that the two were viewed in the same way and used in the same way. Both stones and water were used for healing purposes and both stones and water were used for worship, but stones were also used to tap into the bounties of the Earth Mother and for looking at the seasons. Magic has been seen to be made from both and magic can still be made if we allow it to be.

The Cult of Water

In this day and age it is possible for the vast majority of people to turn on a tap and out will gush water. Not, in my view, water that possesses any powers for it is contaminated with far too many chemicals; but water nevertheless. There is little magic and mystery about this life-giving liquid any more. It is taken for granted. And only when the Water Boards or whatever they decide to call themselves these days, impose a ban on the use of hosepipes so our pretty flowers cannot be watered and our fine lawns cannot look as green as we would like do we start to miss water. No-one in this country will die through being unable to partake of water. After all, we are an island and islands usually attract a great amount of rainfall as well.

Imagine then, if you will, what the people who existed some 5,000 years or more would have thought if the life-giving liquid stopped falling from the sky and the great god of the sun shone brightly up above, drying everything. Food supplies would wither and lakes and rivers would trickle to nothing. Where would they look for their water supplies? At certain places spotted about the landscape the Mother Earth goddess would still provide for her children because water would still spring from rock faces or from the earth itself in a, seemingly, never-ending supply in spite of the drought. Surely, therefore, this was a site to be venerated and worshipped and, surely, if the Mother Goddesses was here then it was not only a life-giving source but it was a place for healing as well? Usually, water springing from within the earth would, obviously, have minerals as part of its make-up and these minerals could very well contain healing properties.

More often than not the sources of these springs or wells would be bedecked with stones – stones that had been brought from short or long distances and in all probability stones that contained a good deal of quartz crystal, the very power that we use for our digital watches and other hi-tec instruments today. There is nothing new under the sun.

So what about the sacred waters and stones of Cheshire? I do not propose to itemise every single magical and mystical stone and every single source of water from the ground but perhaps we can look at a few that are more than worthy of attention. Perhaps, also, you would like to add to the list because they are all around us in this county of ours; we just need to look.

I have already mentioned some qualities of that tract of land upon the escarpment that overlooks the Plain of Cheshire known as The Edge. I have made reference to the modern-day worship that has taken place and I have, hopefully, hinted at the way modern-day legends have been carved out of the landscape there. More importantly, I hope I have shown how the legend of the Sleepers Under the Edge stems from the Celtic legends of Fin or Finn the predecessor of the Warrior King Arthur that in turn stem from the graves or tumuli of the warriors that are upon the Edge. In addition, that area abounds with wells and springs and these are no ordinary wells or springs. Most of them are what we, today, would class as Holy Wells.

Four of them are more noticeable than the others and for the sake of brevity perhaps these are the four that should be looked at within these pages first of all. We shall, of course, journey across the county as well. The first is now nothing more than a hole in the ground surrounded by a wood and barbed wire fence, presumably to keep cattle and other livestock from falling in. It would be sad, indeed, if it had been erected to keep humans out but, then again, safety is foremost today and it may be a necessary evil to have such a fence. It is across the road from a farm that bears the name Bryn Lowe and its very title suggests that there was a burial place there, because the appendage "Lowe" means, or meant, just that. The water from this would not be drinkable today and it is a fact of life that most of the water from most of the holy springs and wells within this county could not be drunk with safety, mainly because of the poisons we scatter over fields in the form of fertilisers, weed-killers and whatever seeping into the water sources. How different and how sweet our water would have been at one time. Over at Wincle, near to Wincle Grange where the monks of Combermere Abbey had a sheep-rearing outpost there is a spring surrounded by stones that have obviously formed, at one time, a sort of amphitheatre presumably to accommodate the vast numbers who would have journeyed there to partake of the healing or holy water. This place now has the name "Honeyfall Well" ... sweet water flowing from the earth.

But to return to The Edge. The most famous well upon that escarpment in this day and age is undoubtedly the one we now call the Wizard's Well. Park your car at the first lay-by on the left after you have climbed the road from Alderley Village and the quaint fingerpost says "To The Edge". Walk towards Castle Rocks where Master Masons employed by the Earls of Chester started to build a defensive castle then had second thoughts and take the footpath that bears to the left. Within a short distance there is a sandstone outcrop and a stone trough beneath it. This trough has been concreted at some time and water seeps from the rock face into it. The overflow is now carefully carried away so that the oft-used footpath will not get too muddy. Above this there is a carving of a face that has been made to look like a wizard, presumably Merlin, and there is some comparatively recent carving that invites you to "Drink of this and take thy fill for the water falls by the wizard's will." All very nice and quaint and something to perpetuate the legend that has spawned on the Edge of the Wizard and the Knights sleeping under the Edge. It's good for the tourist trade and certainly the person who carved that in late Victorian times intended that the myth should live on. I have been told who actually did this carving and I believe that his descendants have now gone public and told the world also, but this is not the place to delve into a whodunit. It was done for good reason, just as the circle of stones upon the Edge and known as the Druid's Circle was erected at the same time and for the same reason.

I wonder, in fact, whether the so-called Wizard's Well was carved not merely to make the Merlin myth more tangible but to keep people away from the actual holy, magical and mystical wells that really do exist in the area? If this was so then that stone carver did a great service because Victorian and post-Victorian piety was out to destroy or to subdue anything that could be classed as un-Christian and perhaps the two holy wells of the Edge would have been no more, who knows?

So where are these two holy wells and what are they all about?

Again, they are easy enough to find and are marked on the Ordnance Survey maps with the letter W although a visit to the National Trust information office behind The Wizard Hotel will only produce the information that there is a holy well apart from the Wizard's Well. The easiest way of explaining how to get to them both is to park at the lay-by by Beacon Lodge and walk into the woods. Take the left hand path and before you know it you have arrived at well number one. Take the spiralling path from here and within seconds number two is within view.

This is the place that dreams are made from. Both wells are within an area that is surrounded by oaks and, more importantly, yew trees. These are the descendants of oaks and yew that undoubtedly formed part of a Grove, a Druidic Grove. This is the heart and soul of The Edge and is much a part of the Sleepers Under The Edge saga as Fyn the Celtic Warrior Chief and much more. Here is the stuff of legends and here is, in all probability, the finest remaining example of a Sacred Grove in the entire county of Cheshire. There are others – there is one at Fools Nook and there has been one at Malpas and one at Bunbury and the Peckforton Hills still hold clues to the Druids of old – but in spite of everything, The Grove at The Edge is still pretty much intact.

Yew trees were venerated by the Celtic holy men, as were oaks. Oak was the life-giver to the sacred mistletoe. A Druidic Grove, where healing and ancient arts were carried out and also sacrifices were made to three Celtic gods: the high and mighty Esus, whose victims were usually hanged from sacred oaks; Taranis the god of thunder whose sacrifices were burnt alive in wicker figures or cages and Teutates, the favourite god whose sacrifices met their fate by drowning at Celtic holy sites such as wells or pools.

Here, perhaps, we can deviate just a little before returning to the wells of The Edge, for not so very far away at Lindow, the Celtic Black Pool, there was discovered the now world-famous "Lindow Man" or "Pete Marsh" as he was nick-named. This was a sacrificial victim of the Celts and this was a sacrificial victim that, I believe, had made his way from The Edge to Lindow Common where he met his fate. Before being ritually garrotted (shades of the Cheshire Smile and the Cheshire Cat) he would have been anointed with water from a holy well. The holiest site I am aware of within these parts would have been on The Edge for here was a very, very special place indeed. Here was the place that the warrior chiefs were buried and where the holy men conducted their special ceremonies and just down the road at Lindow in the sacred Black Pool the sacrificial victim met his fate. For the whys, hows and wherefores I can heartily recommend Ann Ross and Don Robins' exceedingly well researched *The Life and Death of a Druid Prince* (Rider, 1989).

How well I remember being tipped off about the fact that a body had been discovered at Lindow and how well I recall the frantic efforts of Cheshire police to get to the bottom of the mystery. There was a buzz of excitement, especially when it began to dawn on everyone that the discovery was of world-shattering importance. They certainly fathomed the mystery in record time and, for good measure, they solved another murder along the way as well.

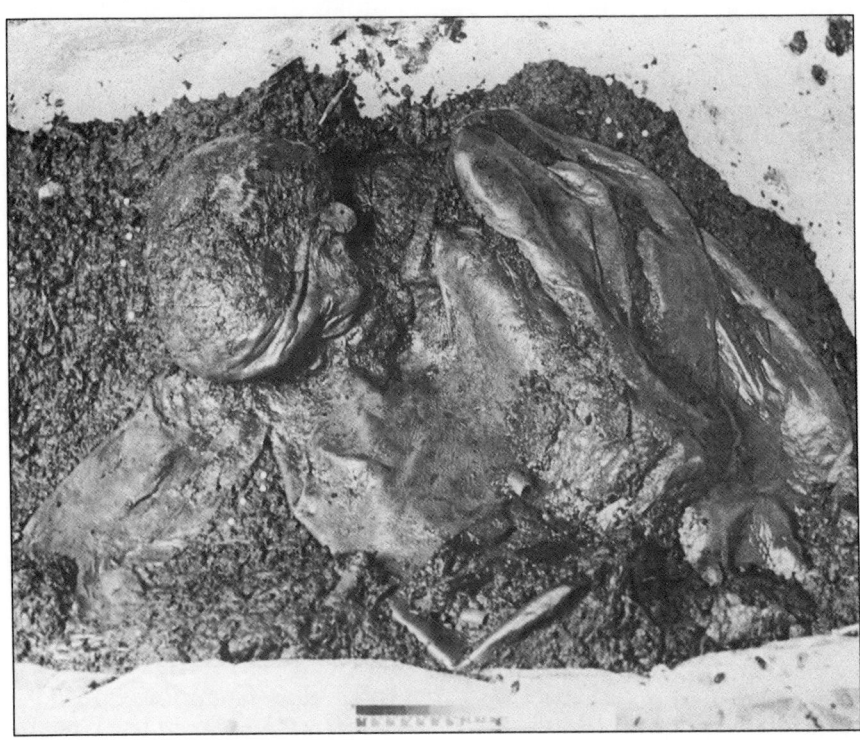

Lindow Man, the body found in peat at Lindow Common. Was this connected with the Celtic holy shrines at The Edge?

But let us return to our two wells. The top one of the two still has marks in the rock that clearly indicate there has been a carved head there at some time. It has been removed and may very well form an ornamental centre-piece in someone's garden now. At one point in the history of the site there can be no doubt that where the stone head was placed above the holy water there would have been an actual human head or skull. This was exceedingly important to the Druidic beliefs of the time and the Celtic Cult of the Head can still be seen in practice with the stone head carvings that adorn the gable ends of many buildings throughout Cheshire. The famous Image House at Bunbury was undoubtedly adorned by a number of these heads but where those came from is a mystery. There are two stone "troughs" at this site, one much smaller than the other and they are very intriguing.

Some time ago my friend Maurice Winnel and I were looking around this holy well and were joined by two elderly gentlemen who were walking with a spaniel dog. We got to talking and one of them said that he remembered visiting here with his grandfather some seventy or more years ago and he was told at the time that the larger of the two troughs was known as the Healing Well and the smaller was known as the Holy Well.

"What do you know about the Wizard's Well?" asked Maurice.

"That's just a few feet away, around the corner" said the gentleman.

Now this seemed very odd because the site known as the "Wizard's Well" is quite a distance from this site and the other well just around the corner had never, as far as we were aware, been known as the Wizard's Well. He must have been mistaken and got the two mixed up, we thought.

Or had he?

"Are you sure?" I asked.

"Oh yes, that's the Wizard's Well, my grand-dad always said that."

We left it there.

Maurice Winnell at the Holy Well and Wishing Well, The Edge. This is within what could once very well have been a Sacred Grove. There are oaks all around and also yews. The path from another sacred well winds clockwise to it. On the rockface can be seen where a carving of a head used to be.

But it set us wondering. The second of these two Holy Wells is, again, something rather special. Behind it is a cave and I would imagine that this cave has been occupied by a holy person, perhaps an Anchorite or Hermit, placed there to watch over the Holy Water and Well. The local tradition now has it that behind the rock face at this spot are the Iron Gates that are said to be protecting the Knights sleeping under the Edge and, like every good modern myth, there is someone who knows of someone who has seen them. Was this gentlemen whom we had spoken to while he was out walking his dog confusing the Iron Gates myth with the Wizard's Well myth? Or was his grandfather correct and this was indeed the original Wizard's Well? The name Wizard could have been applied to either a Celtic Druid or a Holy Man or Healer (possi-

The most dramatic evidence remaining of a Celtic holy site on The Edge. This well is in front of a cave presumably once housing a hermit or holy person to guard the sacred spot. The cave could in all probability have been looked upon as the womb of the Earth Mother. This is where Hilary "saw" babies being placed into the holy water ... a pre-Christian baptism, perhaps, at the Mother's Womb? She also "saw" people in blue robes. The Celtic wise men known as Ovates wore blue robes.

bly a Hermit) and had the "new" Wizard's Well been carved to keep people away from the real one?

So there we have it. Please visit this Holy Site where the two wells are to be found but respect what it has been and what is still is. Here is the true magic and mystery of The Edge.

Healing waters

About eight miles from Chester is the charming village of Burton, now declared a conservation area. There is a feeling of well being about this place and there always has been, it would appear because on the edge of the Dee Estuary marshes there was, some 700 years or so ago a place where, it has been said, sick people and those who were dying were sent. This "hospice" was a centre of healing. The tiny headland called Burton Point was at one time in history the site of earthworks. It has been suggested they were connected with the defence of the port but the name "Burh" from which Burton takes its title means a defensive mound, earthwork or other structure – as does Prestbury. And delightful Burton is also the site of a Holy Well. The Domesday book records that there was a priest at Burton but makes no mention of there being a church. Perhaps the church had been laid to waste by the Normans or perhaps there was no church at all. Perhaps the priest was in fact a Holy Man in charge of the Holy Well. It was at one time known as Patrick's Well, presumably after St Patrick, and here we are again returning to the Celtic sources of water worship for St Patrick's Celtic connections are legendary. It is a spring that is now known as Hampston's Well situated on Station Road just outside the village. Obviously it has been used as a source of drinking water and at one time it was forbidden to wash clothing in it and every male member of the community had to participate in an annual ritual of cleaning it otherwise they were fined. Obviously a very important place at one time. It was allowed to get into a sorry state but I'm pleased to say it has now been given a spring clean and looks good.

One of the furthest outposts of Cheshire is Winwick north of Warrington and some mile or so to the north of this village at

Hermitage Green is a well known as St Oswald's Well. It is, in fact, on land owned by Woodhead Farm and as such is on private property. Please respect this. The nearby church is also dedicated to St Oswald and this Northumbrian King was slain at the Battle of Maserfield in 642 AD. The story is told that as he lay on the battlefield he scratched the soil and where he disturbed the earth water began to flow and this is the site of St Oswald's Well. Surprise, surprise, this water was found to have healing properties and for countless years pilgrimages were made to the site by sick people just as they go to Lourdes today. As recently as 1988 a procession went to the well and a Christian service was held there. I sincerely hope this practice is kept alive for our ancient healing wells and the traditions surrounding them must not be lost. They are part of the very make-up of Cheshire people. This area was used to bury Bronze Age people's venerated dead, as well, because there is a Lowe or Barrow nearby and later the Christians utilised it also. They were certainly burying their dead their in the year 700 AD.

At Timbersbrook underneath Bosley Cloud, there are some stones known as Catstones from which a brook springs and here, also, the water has been venerated. The name Catstones comes, it is said, from the worshipping of the "Cat Goddess". A possibility and perhaps yet another explanation of the Cheshire Cat, but these stones also look like a cat and so, perhaps, the name comes from this. The word "Cat" also denotes the site of an ancient battle.

Today, Wildboarclough Water is bottled and enjoyed by thousands of people as a refreshing drink. The same could have been said many hundreds of years ago for people used to journey into the hills there to partake of the waters. The Clough stream is also the reason for the area getting its name, as I describe in my book *Magic, Myth and Memories*. This is the Land of the Wild Bore, not the wild boars.

Majestic Mow Cop, straddling the borders of Cheshire and Staffordshire, emits healing waters. There are numerous wells and springs coming from the rocky fissures and this area has been a place used by people for religious purposes for thousands upon thousands of years. I do not think it any coincidence that the Old Man of Mow, the rocky outcrop resembling a man, has looked at many and varied religious ceremonies for thousands of years.

People have been attracted there because of the special feel of the place and because of the curative properties of both its stones and its waters. Many years ago, far more than I care to tell, I walked up that hill with my mother who was going to look at a public house named the Oddfellows because she and my father were publicans and were thinking of taking over the premises. This is the pub that straddles both Cheshire and Staffordshire and at one time, when closing times were different in the two counties, customers would go into another part of the building to have extra drinking time. As we climbed the steep hill towards the Oddfellows we were greeted by a lady who invited us into her house. The day was hot and sunny and the hill climb was making us sweat.

"Have a drink of the finest water you'll ever taste" she invited. And we did. It tasted wonderful, there was a hint of a sparkle and there was also a taste of water. Yes, pure water does have a taste of its very own, but unfortunately chemicals now hide that from us, but pure water is the most refreshing drink there is. It is Nature's Own Adam's Ale.

The Roman road of Watling Street passes through Kelsall to the salt towns of Cheshire. It is supposed this road was constructed purely for the collection of salt for the salaries (salarium) of the Roman soldiers but this road was there long, long before the Romans came to our shores. It is an ancient track used by man for many centuries before the invaders. The Romans merely took it over and improved it. There are several springs within and around Kelsall that have a high mineral content and they have been credited with providing good health and long lives to residents. The area was a defensive spot used during the Bronze Age and before and there is still to be seen the remains of a Bronze Age fort on Kelsborrow Hill. I think this should be Kelsbarrow and it denotes a burial place also.

In the Peckforton Hills, there is a spring gushing from the rocks that is as cold as ice and has been used for healing purposes for as long as man has been on the planet. Coincidentally, as I write this I have heard on the radio of a new treatment for rheumatism that involves the immersion of the affected joints into ice-cold water. Perhaps, as I have said before, there is nothing new under the sun. T.A. Coward's *Cheshire* of 1932 mentions that the water shines like silver. At one side near where the water gushes out of the rock a metal plate had been affixed recording, in Latin, its curative properties and that it was made or owned by Daniel Jackson in 1624. There are a number of stone pipes that have obviously been used to carry the water and a large, hollowed, stone that appears to be the well head. A hollow in the rock wall, through which the water at one time may have entered, suggested to Mr Coward "the shrines or decorations of holy wells which are common in other parts of the country" and he wondered if there was any record of a medicinal spring here in pre-Reformation days.

In 1757 the Rev William Cole visited the site with the Vicar of Tarporley, Mr Allen, and he described it as follows:

"In this parish under the great hills of Peckforton and Beeston is a most pleasant cold Bath, which issues out of the Rock into a Bason of the same ... . It goes by the name of Horsey Bath and going thither Aug: 2, 1757, one Morning with Mr Allen who made use of it for the Rheumatism, the Clearness and Limpidness of the water tempted me also to go into it: and tho', out of Refreshment I have all my life constantly in the Summer Time 2 or 3 Times a Week gone into the River to bath, which would, as I thought, have sufficiently inured me and hardened me to any cold Bath: yet on my plunging in I found my Mistake in the great difference of a common River and this cold Bath, where I could barely stay in one Minute, during which Time the Coldness of it was so extreme, that trying to speak, found it out of my Power."

Power of the White Water

I must tell the tale of Spurstow Spa or, rather, how Hilary and I attempted to find Spurstow Spa.

It was one of those delightful Sunday mornings that only Cheshire can provide. As we drove through villages and along country lanes the church bells rang and the sleepy cows began to chew again. All was right with the world and we were setting off to visit Spurstow Spa, a spot that has been used for, probably, thousand of years, to cure thousands of people. The only problem was that although countless thousands had visited there in the past and there were clearly defined trails to it on the Ordnance Survey maps, life is never that easy today.

Spurstow Spa lies in the middle of Bath Wood just outside Spurstow itself and the very name given to that wood suggests that the site has been used by people for bathing. The water that comes from the ground has a high salt content and became known as "Spurstow White Water" and has long had a high reputation for its curative powers. There was once a signpost that read:

If you are troubled with sore of flaw,
This is the way to Spurstow Spa.
If all your sores you've left in the lurch,
This is the way to Bunbury Church.

We parked just by Bath House Farm first of all, because the map showed a footpath from there to the spa. However, the footpath sign was pointing along the road towards Haughton Moss, and definitely not in the direction we wished to go. The easiest way out of this dilemma was to move to another path and so we drove a little way to Peartree Farm. As we followed the footpath sign we found ourselves heading straight towards the farm building itself and were met by a charming couple, obviously the owners of the property, and I bade them "Good Morning".

"Can you point us in the direction of the footpath to Spurstow Spa?" I asked and was told that although the footpath on the map appeared to, in fact, go directly through the building itself there was little point in trying because we would be met with a stone wall, although the offer was certainly made if we so wished. Of course we did not seek to take up the offer and the gentleman advised us to walk around the building in the fields. This we did and endeavoured to keep to where the map showed the footpath to be and headed towards Bath Wood. Here we came across another difficulty for the footpaths sign clearly showed that the path led through the wood but the way was blocked by all manner of overgrown undergrowth. There were fallen branches, bramble bushes, heather and everything that Mother Nature could throw up to prevent anyone passing through. I sincerely hope that since our expedition into darkest Cheshire this has been rectified to everyone's satisfaction. It is not a journey I would recommend for the faint hearted and, indeed, it now seems that the spa itself, or rather what is left of it, is surrounded by a barbed wire fence. I cannot and must not encourage anyone to visit this spot, I fear, because it seems now to be on private property. A great shame and something I will refrain from commenting upon. However, thanks to the wonders of present day telephoto lenses I was able to come away with some photos of what remains. Nearby is Hollywell House and I wonder if, at some time, this was in fact Holy Well.

All that remains of Spurstow Spa. This site was for centuries a place of pilgrimage and of healing. Now it is a weed-infested bog with a few pieces of rusty scrap iron strewn about. The scrap looks like part of a boiler and could have been used to extract brine.

And finally, we can't forget the legendary wishing well at Gayton on the Wirral. It was thought that anyone who made a wish and threw a stone backwards into the well would realise their desire. This was true of many wells and waters within Cheshire and throughout the land and stems from the practice of offering sacrifices or giving offerings to the gods or spirits of the water.

Egerton Legh wrote:

> *The Wishing Well, the Wishing Well,*
> *In Gayton lane you find;*
> *Oft had I of the spring heard tell,*
> *Sought by fond maid or hind.*
> *Should ought fair maid long to have,*
> *Shew flies to this lone spot;*
> *She throws a stone into the wave,*
> *Then seeks again her cot.*
> *She fancies as the bubbles rise*
> *Above the sinking stone,*
> *Her wish must realise the prize*
> *For which she left her home.*

Rivers of Life and Death

Rivers possess the power of life and, as such, they must possess a god, goddess or spirit. So thought our ancestors and the magical qualities of our Cheshire rivers was something held in awe.

The River Dane, named after the same Celtic deity who gave her name to the River Danube, was such a river. At Dane Bridge, Wincle, there is still a pool where it is thought sacrifices were made to the river goddess and there is a path, believed to be a ceremonial path, that goes from there to a rock known as Hanging Stone.

The River Dee has long been known as the Magical River or the Wizard's Stream, among other descriptions. It has associations with the magical powers of the Celtic Druidic figure of Merlin from its origins within Wales and its ebbing and flowing has been used as a means of divination.

Spenser makes mention of the Dee in two passages of the poem "Faerie Queen". In one he takes note of the source of the river in connection with Merlin and in another makes special mention of its charm.

Another poem, referring to the mystical properties given to its movement, says:

> *Twice under the earth her crystal head doth run:*
> *When instantly again Dee's holiness begun,*
> *By his contracted front and sterner waves, to shew*
> *That he had things to speak might profit us to know;*
> *A brook that was suppos'd much business to have seen.*
> *Which had an ancient bound 'twixt Wales and England been,*
> *And noted was by both to be an ominous flood,*
> *That, changing of his fords, the future ill or good*
> *Of either country told, of either's war or peace,*
> *The sickness or the health, the dearth or the increase;*
> *And that of all the floods of Britain, he might boast*
> *His stream in former times to have been honour'd most.*

The River Weaver at Barnton from an old postcard (W.Gee). This river rivalled the Dee for magic associated with it. There is, I understand, a statute still in existence that states it is illegal to swim in the river on a Sunday. The punishment could be deportation..

Such, too, has been the case with the River Weaver, another river given mystical powers by our ancestors. The Weaver obtains a prominent place in consequence of its close connection with the production of salt at "those two renowned Wyches, the Nant-Wyche and the North". Salt is used in sacrifices. Salt is a token of friendship. Thus the Weaver became another holy river, a rival to the Dee. It became possessed, as it were, of a rival sanctity and the poem adds:

And bare his name so far, that oft 'twixt him and Dee
Such strife there hath arose in their prophetic skill."

The Roman altar to the Water Nymph discovered at Great Broughton near Chester.

In 1875, according to the Dean of Chester, the Rev J.S. Howson, the relation of salt to health is introduced as another element in the Weaver's claim to holiness. He wrote that the "healthful virtues" of the Weaver were such that even the Sea Gods had recourse to the river for "physic in their need" and that by "his salts he durst assure recovery."

At Chester, a Roman altar was uncovered that was dedicated to the nymphs and fountains, an obvious reference to the cult of water worship so very much alive within the Roman legionaries.

Its discovery was made on the 29th of March, 1821, in a field known as the Daniels in Great Broughton and it was then the property of a gardener called Simon Faulkner. It was near to the crossroads of the major Roman, and pre-Roman, roads to Manchester and Chesterton about 350 yards from a pub called the Black Lion. Some workmen were getting sand for building at Eaton and were levelling a tumulus about half way up the field when they uncovered the altar.

This religious object was discovered on the site of an ancient burial mound and close by a crossroads – a mystical spot of great significance. It was surely no coincidence that the Romans chose to place the shrine to the goddesses of the water at the same spot that Neolithic man had chosen to bury his venerated dead. This must be a special place indeed.

Magic of the Stones

Before we leave Cheshire we must look at some stone magic within. Straddling the border of Staffordshire and Cheshire there is the desecrated, destroyed and dilapidated example of a chambered long cairn known as The Bridestones. I fear I would be repeating myself too much if I went very far into the whys and wherefores of this site because three other books of mine have drawn attention to this spot, an elegance of sufficiency. This is the shrine to Bridgit the Earth Mother and is, or was, a fertility site remembered up until very recent times by virtue of young men and women going there to be married "over the brush" and, although not married in the eyes of the church certainly married in the eyes of the Earth Mother.

This is also where couples would go to copulate during the month of May, for it was generally accepted that a child stood a far better chance of survival if born in February or March as it then had the full run of summer ahead of it. This is where I have seen someone reel from the shock of a powerful current as he touched one of the upright stones and this is where I have been told by the person himself of how a flying saucer, UFO or call it what you will rose from behind the site and "abducted" him. For this I would refer you to *Staffordshire: Its Magic and Mystery*.

There is much to explore around that region – there are a

number of earth energy lines concluding there and travelling through and I have been informed of one that travels from the Bridestones to Arbor Low in Derbyshire. I have traced it on the map and also dowsed it on the map but have not followed it on foot with dowsing rods as I like to. Perhaps that can be the subject of a chapter in a future book, who knows?

And then there is the prehistoric village up there, shown to me by my friend Maurice Winnel. That, also, is discussed elsewhere as is the possible connection with the fairy people and the Knights Templars – a concoction indeed.

There are many burial mounds across the county and some still retain their stone markers – just as we have headstones on graves today. One is near the summit of Toot Hill (and is surrounded by a fairy ring) and another is at Langley and is visible from the road.

Sandbach is famous for its Saxon crosses that stand in the town centre, but there are others in Sandbach that are of equal, possibly greater, importance. They are bits and pieces that remain of monoliths that were, presumably, destroyed by Puritan zeal. Some may be of pre-Christian origin. They can be found in the churchyard.

Three stone uprights brought down from Macclesfield Forest now stand in West Park, Macclesfield, while a similar one is still in situ on top of a huge man-made mound at Clulow Cross and yet another lies in a hedgerow at Upton Priory on a ley line from Prestbury to Gawsworth churches. Two more identical ones lie just over the border in Staffordshire in parts of that county that were, at one time, in Cheshire. One is at Knight's Lowe at Swythamley Hall and the other is in Leek Parish Churchyard.

The Bowstones above Pott Shrigley are almost intact and their name suggests they were "bowed" to out of veneration, although tradition has it that this is where arrows were fired and sharpened.

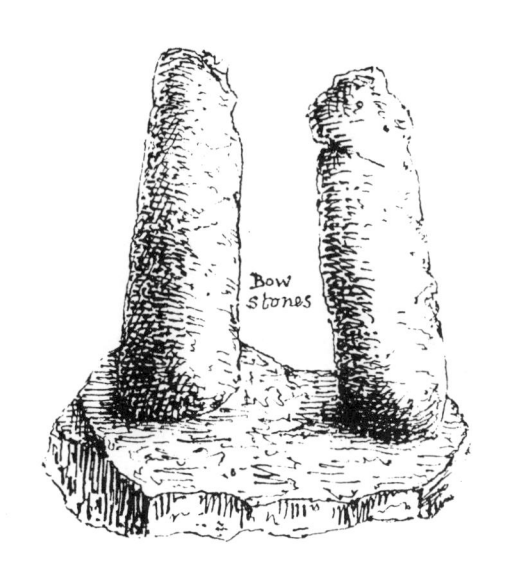

A drawing of the Bow Stones.

There are several boulders in Cheshire that mark crossroads or paths of energy. One such stone can be found at Malpas and there is another just out of Malpas by the side of a roadway in the wall of a farm that is on an earth energy line that we discovered as we were driving towards the "Dragon Line" that travels through Dragon Hall.

Thurstaston, it is said, derives its name from Thor's Stone Town. This may or may not be the case, and there are many who throw cold water on the idea, but there is certainly a stone there dedicated to Thor. Is it, then, too much of a coincidence that this is how it got its name? I for one think that the Town of Thor's Stone is the right derivation but then I suppose I am biased. This stone is a large rectangular rock made from sandstone . Its size varies but is about ten metres wide, about eight high and somewhere in the region of sixteen or so metres in length and possesses a somewhat flat top. Today the sandstone is crumbling, aided in no small way by the many thousands of people, young and old, who have climbed up it throughout the ages. And it is covered in initials and other graffiti. Legend has it that it was a sacrificial stone and this is as maybe. Whatever the reason, it is certainly a stone that has been used for ceremonial purposes and it is certainly a stone that has, because of its very size, been awe-inspiring. I feel it has been a rock used as a meeting point and an assembly for religious and social purposes. Oh, and it is also on a powerful earth energy line as well.

Also on the Wirral, at Bidston Hill, close by the Observatory there is a carving in the rock. In fact there are a number of carvings, some old and some not so old. But one is of enormous interest and shows what is thought to be a "Sun Goddess". The figure has outstretched arms and the head is in the direction of where the sun sets on Midsummer Day. There is also a figure with a Cat's Head and it has the moon at its feet. It has, for obvious reasons, been referred to as the Moon Goddess but here, again, I wonder whether the Cat Head has something to do with a religious cult that most obviously thrived in Cheshire and could have shared its origins with the Cheshire Cat.

On another rock on top of that hill is the figure of a horse and this could well tie them all in with the Celtic religion, for the horse figured prominently within their religion (I feel the legend of the farmer on his way over the Edge at Alderley with a white horse who meets the magician or wizard gives clues to the Celtic origins of that legend, also).

There is much work still to be done in Cheshire and I hope that, one day, you will accompany me on another journey of exploration within this wonderful county. I am conscious of the fact that I have not chronicled everything, I leave that to others, but I sincerely hope that I have whetted your appetite to go out and explore. Cheshire is there for the asking and it will give answers if the right questions are asked.

Please ask those questions.

All that remains of a once proud stone pillar at Astbury. Perhaps it was a "cross" or perhaps it was a stone placed there before the church was built. Like most of the stone "crosses" of Cheshire, it was destroyed by the Puritans.

This stone cross used to stand in the road at Styal. It was hit by a motor car, not surprisingly, and the remains re-erected away from the highway. However, this photograph although extremely old, does not show the original stone pillar at Styal. This is a Christian cross placed there some time during the village's proud history but there would have been a stone much simpler in design. And who can tell the origins of that one?

Index

A

Alder, 16
Alderley Cross, 22
Alderley Edge, 16, 29, 35, 41, 60, 107, 163 - 164
Alderley Park, 14, 22
Alice's Adventures In Wonderland, 2, 8, 10, 152
All Hallows Eve, 2, 4, 59
All Souls Eve, 13 - 14
Antrobus, 11 - 13, 105
Antrobus Soulers, 1, 4 - 5
Appleton, 21
Appleton Thorn, 16, 19 - 20
aquastats, 110
Arthur, King, 108, 116, 163
Astbury, 29 - 30, 127, 183
Audlem, 50

B

Baal, 38
Bards, 26
Barnton, 177
Barrow Hill, 52
Barthomley, 14, 52, 54, 101
Bawming the Thorn, 18 - 19, 21, 27
Beelzebub, 10
Beeston, 38 - 39, 42, 68, 137
Beeston Moss, 31, 67
Beltaine, 4, 26, 38
Beltaine Fires, 38, 41, 43
Bidston Hill, 155, 182
Black Dogs, 156
Black Prince, The, 1, 8, 10, 12 - 13
boggarts, 3 - 4, 81
Bollin, River, 90
Bollington, 25, 40
Bosley Cloud, 41, 161
Boughton, 73
Bowstones, The, 161, 180
Bramall Hall, 51, 147

Bridestones, The, 41, 161, 179
Bryn Lowe, 163
buggins, 3 - 4
Bunbury, 24, 35, 59, 63, 66, 101, 136, 174
burial mounds, 116
Burton, 170
bushes, 16
Butley Hall, 87
Byrons Wood, 17

C

Carroll, Lewis, 2, 6, 10, 152, 162
Castle Hill, 91
Celtic myths, 4, 12, 26, 12, 105
Cheshire Cat, 2, 152 - 153, 171
Chester, 34, 178
Chester, Earls of, 34
Church Coppenhall, 73, 100
Church Grim, 156
Clulow Cross, 180
Comberbach, 12
Combermere Abbey, 101, 136, 163
Congleton, 16, 21
corn dollies, 69
Crewe Green, 52
Crosses, 35
Cult of the Head, 47, 167
curses, 74
Cut Thorn, 18

D

Dane Bridge, 176
Dane, River, 116, 176
Daresbury, 55
Davenport family, 51
Dee, 34
demons, 4
Deva, 143
Dieulacres Abbey, 129
Dodgson, Charles Lutwidge, see: Carroll, Lewis

185

dogs, 155
Dragon Hall, 123
Dragon Lines, 80, 112, 114
Dragon Paths, 119
dragons, 3, 105, 129
Druid's Circle, The, 110
Druidic Groves, 29, 165
Druids, 26, 30, 38
Dumkins, The, 159

E

Earth Spirit, 2
Eaton, 29, 31, 149
Eaton Souling Song, 29
Eddisbury Hill Fort, 124
Evil Eye, 58, 72

F

fairy mounds, 146
fairy rings, 141
Fairyhough, 141
fertility rites, 43
Findlowe, 115
Fools Nook, 26
Foxtwist Hall, 16

G

Garner, Alan, 107
Gaskell, Mrs, 36
Gawain and the Green Knight, 3, 39, 45
Gawsworth, 102, 115, 149, 181
Gayton, 175
ghosts, 102
Glastonbury Thorn, 18 - 19, 22
Godley Green, 157
Golden Stone, The, 111
Goyt Valley, 101
Gradbach, 41
Great Barrow, 135
Great Broughton, 179
Green Man, 2, 32, 34, 36, 41, 44, 47, 52

H

Hallowe'en, 59
Handbridge, 35
Hanging Stone, 176
Hare Barrow, 118
Headless Woman, 81

Healing Oak, 23
hermits, 169
High Legh, 27
Higher Walton, 101
Hobb Hill, 81, 120 - 121
Hockenhull Hall, 85
Holmes Chapel, 1
Holy Well, 29
Holywell, 121
Hood, Robin, 8, 34
Horn Dance, 8
Horse's Head, 13
Huntington, 103

I

Image House, 52, 63
Ince, 145, 147

J

Jack in the Green, 34, 45, 52

K

Kelsall, 73, 172
Kelsbarrow, 172
Kerridge, 37, 40
Kettleshulme, 71, 141
King Canute, 35
Knot Gardens, 126
Knutsford, 1, 32 - 33, 35 - 36, 43, 45

L

Letter In, 1, 8, 10
ley lines, 180
Lightning Oak, 26
Lindow, 43, 165 - 166
Little Dicky Derry Doubt, 10
Little Moreton Hall, 124
Lord of the Flies, 10
Lud, 116
Lud Church, 48
Lyme, Forest of, 49
Lymm, 13

M

Macclesfield, 68, 91, 96, 127
Macclesfield Forest, 55, 141
Maid Marian, 44
Malpas, 55, 121, 132, 181

Man of the Greenwood, 34
Marton, 23
Marton Oak, 16, 23
May Birchers, 36
May Day, 26, 33, 41
May Queen, 9
May Thorn, 18
Maypole, 34
Mellor Moor, 55
Merlin, 72, 107 - 108, 117
mermaids, 3
Middlewich, 129
Mobberley, 135
monsters, 3
Morris Men, 8, 33
Moston, 3
Moston, dragon of, 129
Mottram St Andrew, 16, 28, 149
Mow Cop, 171

N

Nantwich, 39, 51 - 52, 66, 101, 135
Nether Alderley, 21
Nomansheath, 151

O

Oak Apple Day, 24 - 26
Oak Grove, 26
Oak Leaf Day, 25, 26
Ovates, 169
Over, 147
Over Alderley, 16, 158
Overchurch, 134

P

panthers, 160
Peckforton, 38, 138, 172
Piggford Moor, 64
Pott Shrigley, 154
Poulton, 48
Poynton, 70
Prestbury, 86, 113, 146
Prince of Darkness, 8
Prince of Demons, 10
Puck, 81

Q

Quack Doctor, 10
Queen of Hearts, 2, 8

R

Rainow, 71
Robin Hood, 9
Robin Hood's Pickling Rods, 55
Romanies, 149
Rostherne, 27, 34
Royal Oak Day, 25

S

Sacred Groves, 21, 26, 29
Sandbach, 35, 52, 181
Sanding, 36
Saxon crosses, 52
She Male, 8, 9
Sheila-na-gig, 132
Shocklach, 121
Shutlingslowe, 145
Siddington, 69
Somerford Booths, 141
Soul Gangs, 13, 32, 38, 105
Soulers, 8, 10, 12, 14
Spirit Paths, 109
Spurstow Spa, 173
St George, 80, 115, 124, 135
St Michael, 115, 127, 130
Standing Stone, 84
Stanlowe Abbey, 148
Stoak, 147
Stockport, 73
stone circles, 112, 119, 129
Styal, 184
Sutton, 94
Swythamley, 48

T

Tarn Hills, 38
Tarporley, 29, 173
Tarvin, 13
Tattenhall, 72, 80, 83, 122, 124
thorn tree, 16
Three Shire Heads, 18, 64
Thurstaston, 182
Tilstone Fearnall, 99
Toot Hill, 41, 139, 180
trees, 16
Tweedledee and Tweedledum, 10
Tytherington, 88

U

UFOs, 179
Upton Priory, 180

V

Vale Royal, 147
Venables, Sir Thomas, 3, 130
Virgin Mary, 8 - 9

W

Weaver, River, 177
wells, holy, 163, 168
werewolfs, 3
Weston, 100
White Nancy, 37, 40 - 41
White Rabbit, 2, 8
Wicker Man, 47
Wild Horse, 10
Wildboarclough, 59, 71, 171
Wincle, 103, 141, 160, 163
Winwick, 170
Wirral, 3
Wise Ones, 58, 106
Wistaston Manor, 100
witchcraft, 57, 63, 69
witches, 3, 4, 110
witches, dance of, 62
Witton, 69
Wizard's Well, 110, 164
wizards, 3, 72
Wonderland, 11
Wybunbury, 101

Y

Yew Trees, 29
Yule Log, 14